THE
ORGANIZATIONAL
POLITICS PLAYBOOK

---

50 STRATEGIES TO NAVIGATE POWER DYNAMICS AT WORK

Allison M. Vaillancourt, PHD

The Organizational Politics Playbook: 50 Strategies to Navigate Power Dynamics at Work

Published by Wheatmark®
2030 East Speedway Boulevard, Suite 106
Tucson, Arizona 85719 USA
www.wheatmark.com

ISBN: 978-1-62787-850-0 (paperback)
ISBN: 978-1-62787-851-7 (ebook)
LCCN: 2021900162

Bulk ordering discounts are available through Wheatmark, Inc. For more information, email orders@wheatmark.com or call 1-888-934-0888.

TABLE OF CONTENTS

ACKNOWLEDGMENTS

Many of the chapters in this book contain components of columns originally published in the *Chronicle of Higher Education*. I want to offer special thanks to Denise Magner, my editor, for her wise writing advice and constant encouragement.

A key concept described in this book is the importance of building a diverse brain trust. I am fortunate that mine is comprised of too many wise and generous people to list here. I want to express gratitude to the friends who regularly asked when I expected to declare this project finished.

To Richard, Kaitlin, and Grace—love always.

PREFACE:
"I DON'T DO POLITICS"
IS NOT AN OPTION

Have you ever heard someone say "I don't do politics" with an air of dismissiveness or disgust? Perhaps you have even uttered that phrase yourself and felt good about your proclamation because you are a person who believes in fairness, justice, and the value of hard work. While most of us would like to believe that good things happen to good people who deliver on their promises, act with integrity, and behave responsibly, it takes more than a strong work ethic and long hours to get ahead or even survive in most organizations. The reality is that good things tend to come to those who have honed their ability to navigate organizational politics.

Leadership Caffeine author Art Petty argues there are four universal rules of organizational politics:

1. You ignore organizational politics at your own peril.
2. You engage in the politics of your organization at your own peril.
3. All organizations are political.
4. You need to get over #3.[1]

Petty is right. It is easy to be frustrated or angry about organizational politics, but the ability to navigate them is an essential survival skill in almost any organization.

As an organizational strategist and executive coach with a background in political science, I have worked with thousands of people who have struggled to make sense of the organizational politics that permeate their workplaces. The issues that challenge them tend to be clustered into themes that you might recognize.

Theme 1. "I am not in the 'in crowd,' and I don't know why or what it would take to break in and become an insider."

Theme 2. "I am highly qualified and ready for a bigger or different role, but I can't seem to get ahead, while those who work much less are constantly given new opportunities."

Theme 3. "The people around me argue constantly, withhold information, and take credit for each other's ideas. They often seem to be out to get me and each other."

Theme 4. "I have smart and practical perspectives, but my ideas are constantly ignored or sabotaged."

Theme 5. "The organizational chart at my organization appears to be meaningless, and I can't figure out where decisions are actually being made."

The people who share their stories with me are consistently competent, and many are unusually talented, but a good number of them have something in common. It is a shared belief that it should not be necessary to master the art of organizational politics. In fact, when I suggest some of the common strategies for navigating organizational politics—asking adversaries for advice in order to turn them into supporters, being useful to backstabbers, engaging in strategic self-promotion, or forging coalitions—I frequently receive the same response: "That may work for you, but that sounds like politics. I don't do politics, and I shouldn't have to."

"I don't do politics" is a common refrain among highly talented and educated people who believe their intellectual strengths, technical expertise, and willingness to follow the rules should pave the way for results and recognition. Many believe their "I don't do politics" mantra signals that they are pure and superior to those they view as scrappy, and perhaps unethical, organizational politics street fighters. These individuals may be pure, but they are also naïve because getting ahead or even getting things done almost always requires attending to organizational and political dynamics. Furthermore, it is a myth that a good idea and solid dataset are generally powerful enough to move a proposal forward. Effort, logic, evidence, and data analysis can only take us so far. We must also consider relationships, emotion, coalitions, reciprocity, mutual interests, influence, and formal and informal authority. Getting things done takes much more than competence and clever ideas.

Given all the evidence that exists regarding the importance of mastering organizational politics, why do so many otherwise strategic people shy away from learning to navigate them? I believe it is often related to the faulty belief that engaging in everyday organizational politics requires those who practice them to be nasty and unscrupulous. But here is some good news: navigating organizational politics does not require us to sacrifice our ethical principles, and reframing the way we think about organizational politics may actually help us master them.

In his book *Power: Why Some People Have It and Others Don't*, Jeffrey Pfeffer, a professor of organizational behavior at Stanford University's business school, notes that mastering the tools of power and influence is especially essential inside complex, interdependent organizations where boundaries and hierarchies are not always clear.[2] He is right, but mastering political strategies will serve us well in any kind of organization, no matter the size or complexity. Regardless of where we are, we must pay attention to our environment, determine who has real power, and understand how decisions are made.

As we begin to explore the world of organizational politics, it is essential to understand that using political techniques does not make us evil or immoral. It makes us strategic, and, more importantly, it increases our chances of being successful at work and inside the community, cultural, religious, and social organizations where many of us find connection and meaning. Mastering organizational politics can even help us navigate family dynamics, which can often be more contentious and cutthroat than anything we experience at work.

The ability to make sense of organizational politics is a valuable career and life skill that takes keen powers of observation, superior listening abilities, and the capacity to connect seemingly random bits of information. Unfortunately, there is no organizational politics academy or degree program to build proficiency or mastery, so how are we supposed to figure out how to navigate the often treacherous world of tight coalitions, unwritten rules, and secret agendas?

Spending a few decades in organizations observing undeserving people get ahead and decent people getting taken down is the traditional way to build organizational politics savvy. Repeatedly getting burned by crossing and trusting the wrong people has a way of building our sense of what works and what doesn't, but that can be a brutal way to build political muscles. If you are like many people, you may have tried to develop your political navigation skills by reading books like Niccolò Machiavelli's *The Prince,* a sixteenth-century political treatise that offers guidance on how to tyrannize others and advises that it is safer to be feared than loved.[3] Or perhaps you have scoured Robert Greene's bestseller, *The 48 Laws of Power.* With chapter titles like "Crush Your Enemy Totally," "Get Others to Do the Work for You, but Always Take the Credit," and "Keep Others in Suspended Terror," *The 48 Laws of Power* plays into the widespread belief that navigating organizational politics requires ruthless behavior and comfort with deception.[4] While Greene claims he wrote the book to demystify the dirty tricks of the executives he encountered during several painful years as a Hollywood screenwriter,[5] the 452-page tome can arguably serve as a how-to manual for those seeking to acquire, consolidate, and exploit power. If you have not yet read this book, you should, if only to familiarize yourself with tactics employed by those who are directed by a faulty moral compass. I found the book valuable because I believe we must understand the practices of the unscrupulous so as not to be duped by them. While the book is elegantly written and includes an impressive number of historical citations, it is not an action guide for those who consider themselves to be good people in need of some practical guidance about navigating the political landscape at work or inside their community organizations. That is why I wrote *The Organizational Politics Playbook.*

For years, I have been on the hunt for a book that would help people I like to avoid many of the political gaffes I have made or observed during my own career. I have longed for a book with easy-to-read chapters that I could gift wrap for new professionals or send with a "thinking of you" card to those who have been scorched in one organizational drama or another. Unable to find a book that suited my purposes, I decided to write my own.

We will cover fifty strategies for navigating organizational politics in this book. Among them are uncovering the sources of power and influence, helping others look good, understanding the dynamics of organizational change, using connections as a shield of armor, embracing impression management, and creating a sense of value through scarcity. While this book will address predictable strategies such as creating fear, using coercion, and engaging in manipulation, it will do so not to encourage you to use such ploys but to help you recognize them. We must know the dirty tricks of politics in order to combat them. I truly believe we can navigate organizational politics ethically and kindly, and I will show you how.

UNDERSTANDING POWER DYNAMICS

KNOW WHAT IT MEANS TO BE "POLITICAL"

Attempting to undermine rivals, backstabbing, bargaining, building power bases, coalition building, game playing, ingratiation, scapegoating—these are among the concepts commonly cited when people inside organizations are asked to describe activities associated with organizational politics.[1] If this is how most people view organizational politics, it is no wonder that so many of us assume that we must be underhanded, unethical, and energized by divisiveness to survive in highly political organizations.

Navigating organizational politics can be challenging, and the need to do so can increase anxiety and job dissatisfaction while decreasing commitment to the organizations in which we work or volunteer.[2] There is also research to suggest that when an organization is known for being "political," it is less appealing to job candidates and tends to attract a higher-than-average percentage of job seekers with Machiavellian tendencies.[3]

While some of the people who practice political behavior are unethical, surviving in highly political environments does not require sacrificing moral principles. It is absolutely possible to be both ethical and politically savvy—and this book is designed to show you how. But before we get started, we need to be clear that engaging in politics does not make us bad people.

3

There is a joke that the word "politics" comes from the Greek words "poly," meaning "many," and "ticks," meaning "bloodsucking parasites," but the word actually has more admirable origins. The word "politics" emerged from Aristotle's writings and refers to affairs concerning the community. His book *Politics* describes how communities should be governed for the best interests of their citizens, and this includes finding productive ways to resolve competing interests.[4] Several centuries later, political scientist Harold Laswell described politics as "who gets what, when, and how,"[5] suggesting that organizational politics are simply a process for moving things forward.

Because decision-making based on logic, evidence, or clearly stated performance metrics may not work when interests are in conflict, behaviors and influence tactics that we consider to be "political" often arise. When we consider organizational politics as "informal, unofficial, and sometimes behind-the-scenes efforts to sell ideas, influence an organization, increase power, or achieve other targeted objectives"[6] and view political skill as "the ability to effectively understand others at work, and to use such knowledge to influence others to act in ways that enhance one's personal and/or organizational objectives,"[7] we are able to view political behavior as something we can actually master to advance honorable objectives.

An important lesson that I hope you will take from this book is that if we commit to acting with integrity, engaging in organizational politics does not make us evil or corrupt; it simply makes us strategic and better able to advance ideas and complete projects. Leadership and change expert John Kotter has asserted that mastering organizational politics is essential for us to get things done when working with others. In his book *Power and Influence*, Kotter notes that when we are politically astute, make an effort to cultivate strong relationships, and build a reputation for being credible and reliable, we are able to access information and move things forward more easily than others who have been less strategic about cultivating their political skills.[8]

So, having established that engaging in organizational politics is often necessary and that we can engage in political behavior in an ethical manner, let's get to work understanding what we mean when we say that someone has strong political skills. To do this, let's look at five key domains of organizational politics: image management, networking ability, apparent sincerity, social astuteness, and interpersonal influence.[9,10]

Organizational politics domain 1: Image management

Image management is the process used to influence how we are perceived by others. The words we use, the clothes we wear, the positions we take, and the relationships we form all influence how others see us. Those who actively engage in impression management often attempt to cultivate a certain persona to advance their goals and interests. For instance, a wealth manager may join nonprofit boards and volunteer once a month in a local food pantry as a strategy to appear committed to being more than about making money. A welder may talk incessantly about the books he reads to signify that he is an intellectual at heart. A network engineer may dress better than her workplace peers to signal that she is ready for a bigger role. And a struggling small-business owner may lease a car he can't really afford to project an image as a successful entrepreneur. In his book *The Presentation of Self in Everyday Life*, sociologist Erving Goffman likened impression management to being onstage. The person we are while performing for an audience is not always the person we are backstage.[11] The same is often true for those engaged in active impression management.

It is worth noting that impression management is not always a benign activity and may also include taking credit for the work of others or actively working to destroy the credibility of a colleague in order to elevate oneself. We will review a variety of impression management strategies later in this book.

Organizational politics domain 2: Networking ability

Politically adept individuals are intentional about forging and cultivating relationships with a diverse set of people. They invest time to get to know influential people as well as those who may not have influence but have valuable skills, hard-to-find expertise, or access to critical resources.[12] They know that the departmental receptionist may have information as vital as the chief financial officer. They also recognize the value of forging alliances with individuals throughout their organization and even outside of it. Individuals with broad and deep networks are well positioned to use their connections when they require support or need to get things done, and they often benefit from news and updates that are not available to those with narrower connections. Those with networking abilities can call on their connections for advice, connections, last-minute saves, early alerts, and even protection for themselves, their teams, and their friends and colleagues. Employers or political adversaries are often hesitant to take action against those with broad and influential networks because of fear of retribution from influential or vociferous supporters. Want to be safer at work? Start building your network.

Organizational politics domain 3: Apparent sincerity

Those with high levels of political savvy are able to build trust because they are considered genuine and forthright. They seem interested in others and appear not to have ulterior motives.[13] Because the intentions of those with apparent sincerity are deemed honorable, others tend to welcome them into conversations, share information, and demonstrate vulnerability. Building your listening skills, being curious, and honoring your commitments are among the strategies that can be employed to seem sincere. But please don't *seem* sincere. *Be* sincere.

Organizational politics domain 4: Social astuteness

Social astuteness is the ability to read others. It is sometimes called emotional intelligence.[14] Those who possess this ability observe others and are able to determine what matters to them by paying attention to their interactions and behaviors. Interestingly, social astuteness is closely correlated with perceived job performance.[15] Why? Because those who possess social astuteness know what matters most to their supervisors and can present their work in the best possible light. They are also able to create a compelling sense of connection.[16] Talking to a team leader who loves sports? A socially astute individual might suggest "calling an audible" rather than recommending that a team pause to reconsider the current approach. Working with a decision maker who craves recognition as an innovator? A socially astute player will begin her pitch with, "We have the opportunity to be the first in the nation to . . ." Those who are highly socially astute tend to connect especially well with others, and the connections they form often make it possible for them to remove barriers and advance ideas.

Organizational politics domain 5: Interpersonal influence

Individuals with interpersonal influence use charm and charisma to influence others. They put people at ease, are fun to be around, exude positive energy, build rapport, get others to like them, and talk in inspiring ways. Individuals with interpersonal influence can adapt their behavior in response to changing circumstances and connect effortlessly with others. They are highly flexible and know how to calibrate their behavior to align with what others want and expect in order to achieve what they want to accomplish.

As you review these political domains, where do you excel, and where might you need to shore up your abilities? We discuss how to build each of these political domains in the following chapters.

DETERMINE WHO HAS POWER AND WHY

Who are the key influencers in your organization? When troubles arise, who are the go-to people that others visit for guidance? Which manager is known for cultivating exceptional talent? Who is the keeper of organizational secrets? Which organizational members have the largest and most diverse organizational networks?

Navigating organizational politics is made easier when we understand who has power and why. But what makes people powerful? Is it their titles? Their place on the organizational chart? Their budgets? Their networks?

Several leadership theorists have attempted to describe the characteristics that give people power and influence. Early in the twentieth century, German sociologist Max Weber said leaders derive their power from one of three sources: traditional authority, charisma, and rational-legal authority.[1]

Weber described *traditional authority* as that recognized by the sanctity of the tradition of passing power from one family member to another. While he imagined the transfer of power that occurs in countries with monarchies, where kings and queens transfer power to their eldest sons or daughters, a contemporary view of traditional authority may lead us to consider a chief executive officer recommending a succession plan that positions the executive vice president to move into the top role.

Weber's concept of *charismatic authority* is very much alive today. According to Weber, charismatic authority is demonstrated in a leader whose vision, passion, and communication style are inspiring. Me Too movement leader Tarana Burke, Pope John Paul, and Malala Yousafzai, who championed the cause of education for Pakistani girls, each represent charismatic authority.

Weber suggested that *rational-legal authority* comes from organizational structures that offer formal power and authority. Those with this type of power have authority based on their role. State governors have rational-legal authority, as do school principals and nonprofit executive directors.

Later in the twentieth century, social psychologists John R. P. French and Bertram Raven created a more expansive model which suggested that power and influence come from five different sources. No doubt inspired by Weber's model, they advanced one that included legitimate power, coercive power, reward power, expert power, and referent power.

Legitimate power, or position power, is power that is vested in a particular role. It is similar to what Weber classified as rational-legal authority. Assembly-line supervisors, members of Congress, and Internal Revenue Service agents have legitimate power. People generally follow the instructions of those with legitimate power not because they want to but because they have to. Those with legitimate power tend to find it relatively easy to ensure compliance with their wishes as long as they have an official title, but once they step away from their roles or are removed from their positions, they often find that people are suddenly far less helpful. That is because legitimate power can be fleeting. Boards and bosses change, and those who were once powerful can suddenly be left without formal power or even any friends. While legitimate power may feel intoxicating, it is not always enduring.

Coercive power is the power to make people do something against their will. Political leaders such as Vladimir Putin in Russia, Recep Tayyip Erdoğan in Turkey, and Nicolás Maduro in Venezuela come to mind when we think of people who use coercive power. While physical pain or threats of harm may be employed by political despots or neighborhood bullies, coercion in an organizational setting may take the form of threatening an employee with dismissal for failing to follow orders or hinting that key resources might disappear unless an individual demonstrates support for a controversial initiative. Coercive power can be scary because it is mean-spirited and can often be highly unpredictable. In his book *The Power Paradox,* UC Berkeley professor Dacher Keltner asserts that leaders tend to resort to coercive force when their power is actually slipping.[2] So if you notice a leader demonstrating especially manipulative behavior, consider that the actions are being driven by fear. That does not make this egregious behavior forgivable, but it can be helpful to understand the motivation for it.

Reward power is the ability to give other people what they want and may include a *quid pro quo* kind of agreement: "I'll give you this if you give me that." Rewards can also be withheld to ensure compliance: "If you fail to do this, you will be denied that." City council members who approve development deals in exchange for votes and campaign contributions are using their reward power. Philanthropists may use their considerable resources to influence better healthcare and education practices, thereby using their reward power for more worthy purposes. It is a mistake to think that reward power is restricted to those who are wealthy and politically connected, however. By way of example, executive assistants who manage the CEO's calendar have reward power because they can determine who gets access to the key decision maker and who does not.

Expert power is derived from possessing a hard-to-find skillset or knowledge base. The single information technology professional who knows how to restart a system that has gone down has expert power, as does the data analyst who knows how to run regression equations when no one else does. The air-conditioning technician who knows how to keep your twenty-year-old compressor working has expert power, as does your dermatologist. The special events coordinator who knows how to work around the official company policy on catering special events or secure approval for irregular travel reimbursements has expert power as well. The ability to navigate organizational rules is highly valued and can position a person at any level as an organizational-dynamics expert.

Referent power is the power that comes from being admirable or having qualities that others want to emulate. While Weber spoke of charismatic authority, French and Raven used the term "referent power" to describe a more encompassing set of actions and behaviors that so many of us find compelling. When we think of Ruth Bader Ginsburg, Nelson Mandela, or Cesar Chavez, we tend to think of good people guided by a sense of moral conviction, and we admire them for their ethical clarity and sense of focus. Celebrities may also possess referent power as followers aspire to be similarly admired for status and charisma.

Six years after French and Raven published their original model, Raven added *informational power*,[3] perhaps recognizing that access to data and control of it can help influence decision-making. When we have data about market trends and upcoming property sales or even knowledge about who is sleeping with whom, we have power that can be put to use in various ways.

One more form of power should be added to French and Raven's list: *relationship power*. This is the power that comes from having connections with a deep and broad network of individuals who can provide information, advice, and access to others with information and power. Think about the most powerful and influential people you know. Where does their power come from? While we often imagine that individuals at the top of an organizational chart are the most powerful people inside an organization, this is not always the case, especially in organizations where senior leaders turn over frequently. In these kinds of organizations, longer-term employees who know how to get things done can be among the most powerful. Another powerful and protected group of people includes those who make a habit of helping others achieve their objectives.

In his book *Give and Take: A Revolutionary Approach to Success*, Wharton School professor Adam Grant notes that those who are strategically generous tend to benefit from the reciprocity of others. Because they regularly do favors for others, their beneficiaries are inspired to be helpful to them.[4] As you think about cultivating your sources of power, what can you do to help others? Can you make introductions? Offer technical guidance? Explain the unwritten rules?

Power can come from many sources, and certain people have more than one kind of power. Think about the most powerful people you know and consider which sources of power they possess. Next, consider your sources of power and how you might leverage them to reach your goals. Expertise, information, and relationships are increasingly important and can position a person at any organizational level to be especially powerful.

LEARN THE DIRTY TRICKS

Much like good writers have mastered the rules of grammar and syntax in order to artfully break them, savvy political navigators have learned the dirty tricks of organizational politics not because they want to practice them but because they want to better anticipate, navigate, and counteract various maneuvers. Understanding the range of dirty tricks that can be used is critical for personal and professional safety, so a partial inventory of common dirty tricks is provided here. The goal of this chapter is not to encourage you to practice these often unethical political plays but to help you spot them as early as possible. The sooner you recognize that someone is using a political dirty trick, the sooner you can take steps to protect yourself. Here are a few of the nasty moves you are most likely to encounter in almost any organizational setting.

"Accidentally" make a colleague look bad

There are so many interesting ways to embarrass others. One classic strategy involves creating the illusion of being helpful or informative to a coworker or team member in a message that is "accidentally" sent to several others, perhaps in a group chat, "reply all" email, or use of a departmental listserv. Imagine the reaction when several people on an email chain receive a message that reads, "Daniel, your budget document has some pretty serious errors. Let's meet tonight, and I can help you get it in better shape for this week's meeting," which is later followed with, "My apologies, everyone; this was intended just for Daniel." With this, everyone has been put on notice that Daniel is not good with numbers.

Politically manipulative coworkers might also "accidentally" send an incorrect agenda, dataset, or report version to ensure their target is unprepared for a gathering and therefore unable to make meaningful contributions. Failing to provide the promised laptop and projector for an important presentation or giving the wrong link for a Zoom meeting are additional moves designed to make a colleague look unprepared and inept.

Backstabbing

Backstabbing is one of the most common political dirty tricks and involves pretending to be an ally to others while simultaneously trying to undermine them. A backstabber may praise your idea for increasing revenue while having lunch with you but then express concerns about its practicality in a meeting with key decision makers—especially if you are not in the room.

Creating a false enemy

"Don't you hate the way Simran acts like he is smarter than the rest of us?" With an opening gambit like this, your so-called ally Carlotta attempts to get you to weigh in on the many things you find annoying about Simran. It can be fun to have a common enemy, and you may go back and forth for a while, laughing even, as you recount the time Simran spoke with great confidence about the history of the Civil Rights Act, getting wrong both the year of its passage and the president who pushed for it. Later, in a meeting where you and others are gathered to plan a celebration for the anniversary of the Americans with Disabilities Act, Simran will turn to you and say, "I've been told that you think I don't know my American history, so let's have you be on point to prepare all of the background materials so that Carlotta and I can appear informed when we meet with the secretary of labor next month." In this scenario, Carlotta has created a false enemy, and you have been played.

Divide and conquer

When joining an organization or workgroup in which everyone seems to get along, it can be difficult to exert power. Creating friction among team members by offering praise or resources to some, but not all, can be an effective strategy for generating anxiety and creating divisiveness, which make it possible to wrest control of the group.[1] Offering a coveted assignment to a member of the team who is known for being a poor collaborator is a good way to create upset and disorientation, as is unexpectedly providing a very junior person the office with a remarkable view that would generally go to the most senior member of the team. Feigning surprise that certain team members feel that their colleagues are not pulling their weight, even though no such concerns have been expressed, is another example of how to create the tension and internal animosity necessary to destroy trust and camaraderie.

Encourage conformity

"Everyone else is onboard. Do you really want to be the one who holds this up?" The principle of social validation relies on our need to conform to the expectations of others and to go along with the majority opinion so as not to be viewed as an outlier.[2] When you are told everyone else is agreement with a course of action you consider problematic, be sure to check in with the so-called supporters because they may have the same concerns as you do.

Failure by design

This is a strategy whereby an individual is intentionally set up to fail.[3] When a board of directors pressures a company leader to hire a more cautious chief financial officer, the CEO may begrudgingly make the hire and then withhold information that makes it impossible to implement necessary controls or achieve financial stability. In another tactic, a nonprofit foundation leader may bow to pressure to hire a chief equity, diversity and inclusion officer but provide her with a budget too small to deliver on any of her plans and then later condemn her for being ineffective.

The glass cliff

The "glass cliff" is a metaphor that describes the practice of appointing occupational minorities to especially difficult, risky, or contentious leadership roles in underperforming organizations and then blaming them for their inability to turn around an impossible situation.[4] These efforts can often destroy the career of the person given the opportunity, hence the visual image of being pushed off a cliff. If you have been offered a challenge that seems impossible to manage, ask yourself if you are being offered the opportunity because you are uniquely qualified to solve a problem that others can't or if you are being intentionally set up to fail to advance someone else's political agenda.

Go silent

Discontinue communication, cancel meetings, and fail to respond to messages. Be completely and consistently unavailable in order to create insecurity and disorientation.

Information management

Information generally gives people power, and it can be used to influence outcomes, elevate one's status, and even destroy careers. Information management can take many forms and may include gathering secrets that might be used to harm others, hoarding information that others need, releasing negative information at a well-timed moment, or even creating dependence by suggesting that one has ongoing access to vital information that others do not.

Ingratiation

Also referred to as sucking up, or worse, ingratiation is the process of flattering or expressing admiration for a person of influence and perhaps even offering public praise for attributes like their strategic thinking or creativity as a strategy to win their favor. It may also involve opinion conformity, the practice of outwardly agreeing with the opinions, assessment, or behaviors of another to demonstrate interpersonal compatibility.[5]

Lose or be confused by requests

Deny receiving a written request or explain that the request requires further clarification to be executed.[6]

Meeting mayhem

Intentionally show up late for meetings run by your target to disrupt the flow of the agenda once you arrive. Arriving after your target begins a meeting presentation and then asking questions that have already been asked works effectively as well.

Pretend to have insider information

Few things are more disconcerting than feeling out of the information loop. An opponent can be made to feel anxious and uneasy when you suggest that you have regular conversations with an influential venture capital investor or when you say, "Chip is not a fan of a hyper-growth strategy," even though the chief strategy officer goes by "Charles" to everyone and has never actually expressed an opinion about the possibility of pursuing a hyper-growth strategy.

Purge those who came before

This strategy, recommended by Niccolò Machiavelli in *The Prince*, encourages ousting anyone who is not an obvious long-term supporter.[7] A new school superintendent might fire all but the employees who campaigned for him to get the job, or a new college president may wipe out her inherited senior leadership team to ensure that those who report to her are completely loyal and will not cling to old ways of doing business.

Reschedule meetings

Agree to a meeting with someone you do not really want to meet with and then have an assistant cancel it at the last minute with a promise to reschedule it soon. Schedule the next meeting several days or weeks out and then cancel and reschedule again. Repeat this process until the other person gets the message that they are unworthy to meet with you. An even more manipulative approach is to schedule a meeting to "discuss some serious concerns" and then repeatedly reschedule it as a way of making the target anxious.

Require all requests to be put in writing

Make it as difficult as possible to make requests for input, services, or resources by requiring forms to be completed or memos to be submitted in writing. Make the forms as complicated as possible and require detailed justification notes.[8]

Require multiple approvals

Require that multiple people review such things as equipment purchases or salary increases in order to create frustration and discourage future requests.

Scapegoating

The term "scapegoat" refers to someone who did not commit a sin or offense but is offered as a sacrifice to make the community feel better about itself. It comes from the Bible's book of Leviticus, which describes the instructions given to Moses and Aaron about how to select a goat and send it into the wilderness as a symbol for absorbing the sins of others and carrying them away from those who committed the evil deeds. When a university's enrollment numbers are down, the admissions officer may be fired even though a football scandal caused students to choose other schools. Or when a company is sued for sexual harassment, the chief human resources officer may be dismissed for not ensuring that every single employee and manager behaved appropriately.

Blaming employees who are no longer with the organization for missteps made by those currently employed is another example of scapegoating and is useful for deflecting personal blame or accountability. "I would never have committed us to those service terms. I'm pretty sure Chung did that as he was leaving."

Spread false rumors

Spreading false rumors is a tactic designed to harm a reputation or compromise credibility. One might tell a known gossip that you heard your division director is in a drug rehabilitation facility rather than on a thirty-day silent meditation retreat, or wonder aloud whether the top company lawyer will be able to represent the organization well in a planned merger given that you heard through the grapevine she is sleeping with an attorney representing the other firm.

Sow seeds of doubt

Creating concern about one's competence or character is a classic strategy for undermining credibility. Those who practice this strategy raise concerns about problematic behavior but deny personal knowledge of it, relying instead on alleged reports from others to convey the message. You may have heard random utterances such as "Her staff members say she is prone to emotional outbursts, but I've never seen her act unprofessionally" or "His colleagues have suggested that he is overly aggressive when it comes to negotiating contracts, but I think we are lucky to have someone who is so committed to always getting us the most favorable deals possible."

Slow things down

In 1944, the US Office of Strategic Services (OSS), the organization that was the precursor to the Central Intelligence Agency, created what was titled the *Simple Sabotage Field Manual*. This once-classified booklet offered OSS officers guidance for training citizen-saboteurs in other countries to quietly and discreetly disrupt war efforts against the United States during World War II. While the manual offered instructions for causing physical damage to equipment, transportation, and communication systems, the booklet also offered fascinating instructions for disrupting organizations "based on universal opportunities to make faculty decisions, to adopt a non-cooperative attitude, and to induce others to follow suit."[9] The tactics for disrupting foreign governments look eerily familiar to those many of us see almost every day in the organizations in which we work. So what's on that list? Consider the following:

> **Never permit shortcuts.** "Insist on doing everything through 'channels.' Never permit short-cuts to be taken in order to expedite decisions."

Pontificate. "Talk as frequently as possible and at great length. Illustrate your points by long anecdotes and accounts of personal experiences."

Refer all matters to committees. "When possible, refer all matters to committees, for 'further study and consideration.' Attempt to make the committees as large as possible— never less than five."

Bring up irrelevant issues.

Wordsmith. "Haggle over precise wordings of communications, minutes, resolutions."

Reopen decisions. "Refer back to matters decided upon at the last meeting and attempt to re-open the question of the advisability of that decision."

Advocate caution. "Urge your fellow-conferees to be 'reasonable' and avoid haste which might result in embarrassments or difficulties later on."

Express concerns about the propriety of any decision. "Be worried about the propriety of any decision—raise the question of whether such action as is contemplated is within the jurisdiction of the group or whether it might conflict with the policy of some higher echelon."[10]

Vote before voting

When a big decision is to be made and multiple people need to weigh in on the final decision, agree that the majority opinion will prevail and call a meeting to vote on the issue. Prior to this meeting, meet individually with several group members to express concern about what will happen if the vote "goes the wrong way" as a strategy for securing support for your preferred choice. Once the official meeting takes place, do not reference the prior meetings so that it appears the majority came to its conclusion on its own.

It is common to believe that we are overreacting or even imagining things when we are the targets of some of these political dirty tricks, and we may respond by working harder and trying to prove that we are worthy of attention and respect. This rarely works. If you suspect you are being targeted, you probably are, and no amount of hard work is going to turn things around. Succeeding in a highly political environment requires that you be attuned to the range of political dirty tricks that are practiced inside organizations. Navigating in a highly political environment requires the ability to spot the players most likely to practice these political strategies as well as the capacity to devise preemptive steps to avoid becoming a target. In the unfortunate event that you become a target of unscrupulous political behavior, your survival will require you to choose the right political defense.

The chapters ahead offer you advice about how to navigate inside political environments and protect yourself while doing so. These next chapters should also encourage you to consider whether working in highly political environments is right for you. While some people enjoy the drama, intrigue, and constant chess playing that occurs in highly political organizations, others just want to do good work with good people. While organizational politics exist in all organizations, some are more political than others. Knowing your stomach for organizational politics is a key first step in assessing your capacity to navigate them.

SEPARATE THE POWERFUL FROM THE POSERS

A while back, I ordered Sarah Cooper's book *100 Tricks to Appear Smart in Meetings: How to Get by Without Even Trying,* thinking I was purchasing a serious book on upping my professional game. It was helpful all right but not quite in the way I expected. That's because Cooper's advice is actually a comical list of tips and tricks that call out some of our smarmiest and most annoying colleagues. Do the book's strategies actually work? Yes, I have to admit many of them do. Will they keep working once more people have figured them all out? I certainly hope not, and something tells me Sarah Cooper is on a mission to make sure they don't.

Cooper's advice ranges from the best way to make missing a meeting someone else's fault to how to shift power in a room by standing up to draw a senseless Venn diagram. She reveals what slackers and wannabees have known for years: when one is short on substance or smarts, image is everything.[1] So if you need advice about how to subtly claim credit for someone else's work, deftly deflect blame, or appear wise instead of vacuous, Cooper's tutorial is well worth the money.

As I read Cooper's one hundred strategies, I was able to assign names of people who practice many of them in the various circles I travel. There is the copious notetaker who breaks from scribbling only to say, "Ooh, now that is profound" to encourage more idea generation that can eventually be coopted. There is the one who constantly says, "Let me play the role of provocateur here," when even the most banal subjects are up for discussion because he just wants to appear edgy and intellectual. And there is the one who responds to the small-talk question "What's happening in your world?" with, "So, so much, and I hope you understand that I'm not at liberty to talk about any of it right now."

Those of us who have been around for a while know who's got game and who's got nothing, but those less familiar with organizational politics may wrestle to discern who is powerful and who is not. The uninitiated may see Cooper's strategies in action and think they signal genuine status, much like the uninformed believe that organizational charts offer meaningful clues about actual levels of influence. Here are three ways to tell who has real personal power and who is desperate to be considered a player.

Watch where they try to sit

Sitting next to the leader is a common trick used by people who want to signal insider status. Being seated at the right hand of God is considered a powerful and honored position,[2] and sitting to the right of the meeting leader is designed to signal similar status and make it appear that there is a coleading situation that will require in-the-meeting whispering and conferring. When I worked for a university, I watched a colleague regularly show up late and move an empty chair from a perfectly good spot around the table to the space next to the meeting leader as if to suggest "I'm the real one with power here, so now the meeting can officially begin." People who insist on sitting next to the leader may not actually have real power but want to do everything possible to insinuate that they do.

While it is not technically possible to sit at the right hand of the leader during a video meeting, arranging to be the first to arrive and perhaps organizing a brief premeeting before others join lets those who join later know they are not in the inner circle.

Listen for what they know

People with real power tend to have self-confidence and do not feel a need to bluff when they don't know everything. When they are asked to comment on something that is unfamiliar, they say things like "I hadn't heard that" or "Really? That is so surprising." Contrast this to those who want to appear powerful and in the know. They are likely to respond, "I'm not really comfortable sharing on that," or they may close their eyes and shake their head as if to suggest they have deep and top-secret information that is troubling them greatly.

Pay attention to how they make their points

While there are exceptions, people who are confident about their power listen more than they talk. They tend to engage in inquiry rather than advocacy, expressing curiosity about other perspectives rather than attempting to wear down those with opposing points of view. They ask questions—often provocative ones—rather than make pronouncements and minispeeches.

There is a fine line here, of course, between asking provocative questions to enrich a conversation and asking them to highlight one's superior analysis skills. I will admit to volleying, "Are we even asking the right question here?" when I am bored with a conversation or craving attention and recently pledged to stop doing that because it is, admittedly, obnoxious.

Questions that signal a colleague is trying too hard include:

"The trend line is compelling, but where is the regression analysis?"

"I've said it before, and I will say it again: what about our customers?"

"What would the average person in Omaha have to say about this?"

"How do we know any of what we believe to be true is truly actually true?"

If questions seem nonsensical, it is likely that you are not the only one who thinks so, and you might consider responding with "Is this the right question, or do we just think it is the right question?" or "Why Omaha and not Detroit?" The original question asker will be unable to say anything articulate, and you will enhance your own personal status and win the admiration of your colleagues for quieting a blowhard. No, I am kidding. That will not happen. The blowhard will remain a blowhard, and you will look like a jerk for attempting an even well-deserved takedown. Better to try, "You've raised some interesting questions" or say nothing at all, because even powerless people can make for dangerous enemies.

IMPRESSION MANAGEMENT

EMBRACE IMPRESSION MANAGEMENT

Recall the last time you spent time around someone you considered impressive. Beyond the content of what they said, what do you remember about this person's posture, clothing choices, word usage, speaking style, body language, and sense of connection with others? Next, recall the last time you saw someone fumble, lose credibility, or even create animosity in a professional setting. What made the experience so painful? When it comes to navigating organizational politics, impression management is essential, and the chapters in this section provide advice about how to increase your sense of credibility and connection.

Before we move forward, let me acknowledge that impression management is a controversial and often emotional topic. Many of us were raised to believe that skills and hard work pave the way to career success. It is frustrating and disillusioning to discover this is not always the case and that in addition to mastering our technical abilities, we must work on image management to get ahead or even to hold on. Professional-presence books and articles tell us life is unfair and competence will get us only so far. To be taken seriously and to move ahead, we are told that we must strive to look like the leaders who are currently in power.[1] We are supposed to look people in the eye. Check our posture. Use the power of silence. Don't end declarative sentences with what sounds like a question mark. Demonstrate passion. Speak well of others. Admit our failings but not too many.

Appear calm and in control.[2] Women are told to lower the register or their voices but avoid vocal fry at all costs.[3] While explicit instructions about behaving as though one is white, male, and tall are never quite uttered, it is clear that this is the gold standard for executive presence.

In her book *Executive Presence*, Sylvia Ann Hewlett stresses the importance of attending to appearance, communication, and gravitas. I first read Hewlett's book as part of a university book club and recall that group members' reactions to it were decidedly mixed. The conversation began with someone asking whether personal appearance and wardrobe matter as much in higher education as they do in corporate settings. We discussed the fact that one of our most influential professors comes to campus wearing shorts all year long, and several leading researchers wear Hawaiian shirts on most days of the week. "Isn't that evidence that the quality of our ideas matters more than the quality of our haircuts and handbags?" one member asked. Not when you consider that all of the people wearing shorts and Hawaiian shirts are men.

It is worth pointing out that women at this university could not get away with wearing shorts on a daily or even occasional basis because the unwritten rules are different. On most campuses, women must speak well, smile at least occasionally, and dress to a certain standard to be afforded the same respect as men get by just showing up. I may be exaggerating but not by much.

To be fair to Hewlett, she does note that while appearance is the filter by which people judge us, our communication style and gravitas—a sense of charm and presence—matter far more. In fact, there is no getting around the need to demonstrate a sense of grace and connection in any workplace setting. Some would argue that really smart or even brilliant people don't need to be polite or gracious. They don't have to be able to read a room or engage in small talk. But that argument fails to take into account the value and power of social skills to move ideas and agendas forward.

As we continued our university book club discussion, a molecular and cellular biologist agreed that it can be hard to offer counsel about voice pitch, warmth, attire, and interpersonal connections because those things all seem personal and subjective. She noted that scientists, especially, tend to believe their research findings matter more than their wardrobe choices, and she shared her technique of having students evaluate speakers based on attributes beyond the content of the research they are presenting. When students think hard about what makes a speaker effective, she said, they are able to articulate the importance of eye contact, reading a room, speaking clearly, and changing course when a sense of boredom takes hold of the audience.

Discussions about appearance, personal style, and other elements of impression management can often be contentious and drift into spirited debates about the inherent unfairness of societal norms. Is it right to encourage people with smart ideas to look or act in ways that society demands? What if society is wrong for establishing those standards? Does giving such advice serve to perpetuate a system that disadvantages certain populations? If the rules of professional success are unfair, should we be actively engaged in teaching people how to master them?

These are all important and worthy questions that are currently being debated in several settings. I am hopeful that our views of what constitutes executive presence will continue to evolve in ways that are more inclusive. Until that happens, the research is clear that no matter how we talk or what we wear, people are drawn to those who are perceived as both strong and warm.

In 1967, Dr. Martin Luther King Jr. addressed the Southern Christian Leadership Conference in Atlanta. In a speech titled

"Where Do We Go from Here?" King noted, "One of the great problems of history is that the concepts of love and power have usually been contrasted as opposites, polar opposites, so that love is identified with a resignation of power, and power with a denial of love . . . What is needed is a realization that power without love is reckless and abusive, and that love without power is sentimental and anemic."[4]

In their highly readable book *Compelling People*, John Neffinger and Matthew Kohut build on King's theme of balancing power and love and on research conducted by Amy Cuddy and others[5] by explaining why we are more successful when we convey both strength and warmth. "Strength gets things done," they write, and "warmth is what people feel when they recognize they share interests and concerns."[6] To navigate organizational politics, we must appear strong and competent to be credible, and we must appear warm to be relatable. When we are perceived as warm, people are more likely to trust our intentions, and when we are considered competent, we are better perceived as capable of executing our plans. Warmth includes elements such as perceived approachability, friendliness, empathy, kindness, and trustworthiness, while competence is based on demonstrations of intelligence, power, efficacy, and skill.[7]

So how can you convey a balance of both strength and warmth? Begin by using your physical attributes, starting with your head and face. Look people in the eye but not constantly. Nod to acknowledge what is being said. Use a genuine smile that causes crow's feet to form at the corner of your eyes.[8] Next, use your body. Most of us grew up with parents or teachers telling us to straighten our posture as a sign of confidence, but there is more you can do to convey a sense of strength and warmth. Orient your body toward the person talking. If you are sitting, lean forward.[9] When walking, consider the energy you are conveying. Move too slowly and you will be judged as lacking energy or stamina. Move too quickly and you might be considered nervous or disorganized.

Hands are another part of your body that need attention when engaging with others. Those who are politically savvy know that that certain hand gestures can be used to signal confidence, credibility, and connection, while others can be alienating. Research proves that it doesn't take long for hand gestures to cement an impression. In one study, Linda Talley and Samuel Temple videotaped three versions of a male "organizational leader" offering an upbeat one-minute speech about growth opportunities. All versions were recorded in the same location, and the actor wore the same clothes and repeated the same words. The only difference was the use of the actor's hands.

In version one, the actor used no hand gestures.

In version two, the actor used hand gestures commonly considered positive:

Community hands. Positioning the hands as palm face up or vertical to the ground

Humility hands. Clasping hands at chest or waist level

Steepling hands. Forming a steeple with fingertips touching

In version three, the actor used hand gestures that are considered defensive:

Hands in pockets. Having one or both hands in pockets

Crossed arms. Placing one or both arms across the chest

Hands behind back. Clasping hands behind the back

When surveyed after observing one of these three speeches, respondents overwhelmingly reported a greater sense of connection with the man in version two who used positive hand gestures such as community hands and steepling hands.[10] Just as gestures such as crossing our arms can make us seem defensive, pointing, curling fingers into a fist, and using karate chop–like movements to make a point can make us appear angry and should not be used. Fidgeting, clenching, and face touching often signal a lack of confidence and should also be avoided.[11] If pointing feels necessary, you could mimic former president Bill Clinton, who used a thumb point, much to the ridicule of actors on *Saturday Night Live*.[12] Better yet, try a slowly delivered karate chop with fingers curved and your hand slightly tilted upward. And when in doubt, think balls.

Balls? Yes, balls. In their helpful YouTube video, Neffinger and Kohut encourage us to imagine we have a ball in one or both hands. Sometimes it is a volleyball held in both hands slightly away from our body at about waist level, and other times it is a beach ball that can be used for making a bigger point. You may want to imagine a marble-sized ball in one hand while the other hand drops, or you may want to bounce an imaginary golf ball in one hand while the other hands rests at your side.[13]

Once you have your various body parts under control, consider the impression you convey when you enter a room. For some valuable insights, start arriving to meetings or gathering settings early and begin observing how others enter a space. Do they scan the room calmly before choosing where to sit or stand, or do their eyes dart around and signal they are nervous? When latecomers arrive, do they stride in confidently with good posture, or do they tuck in their shoulders and crouch a bit to make themselves seem less visible? Those who manage their images tend to enter a room with poise and confidence even if they are late.

Remember, people are always watching. Like it or not, we are all being judged not only by the quality of the ideas we share but also by our physical appearance and mannerisms. Knowing some of the tricks of impression management can help increase both status and influence.

CONSIDER BEING LIKABLE

Several years ago, my public radio station aired an interview with Don Sobol, author of the *Encyclopedia Brown* series. Sobol talked about his ten-year-old mystery-solving main character and said that one of his most important tasks was making a really smart kid likable to his readers. That caught my attention because I am constantly on the prowl for strategies to help really smart grownups connect better with others.

Many of us work in organizations that give us an opportunity to interact with people who seem to think that being smart trumps being congenial. For the most part, the people who have more intelligence than social skills do not mean to be unlikable; it just doesn't occur to them to make an effort to be pleasant. Their often standoffish or surly behavior prompts others to avoid them, which creates a nasty and perpetual cycle. "They are rude to me, so I have no choice but to be rude to them." I find this sad, but it seems overly forward to suggest that those with limited social skills take a course on emotional intelligence or hire an executive coach. Yet when someone asks for my advice, well, then I get an opportunity to have an important conversation—like the one I once had with one of my former graduate students when she called to ask for career guidance.

My former student was ready to leave her current job but was finding it hard to get a new one. Her experience and talent were not in question, so why did she keep getting interviews but no job offers? The answer, I feared, was that

people found her insufferable. Because the constant rejection had compromised her usual high degree of self-confidence, I decided it would be a bad idea to ask her if she had considered being less of an annoying know-it-all. Instead, I took an indirect route. "How do you think people perceive you?" I asked.

Without having to consider her response, she blurted, "They would say I am spot-on in my analysis, efficient, and generally the strongest member of any group. I am, hands down, the most intelligent. No question."

"So do you have any friends at work?" I inquired next.

"Friends? No, of course not. Those people are really not friend material," she replied.

"You know," I countered, "that might actually be a problem for you." This led us into an interesting conversation about the importance of letting others discover your brilliance rather than offering daily reminders about it and the power of making a game out of being kind when such behavior doesn't feel natural. "Fake nice can actually work," I explained. "At the very least, quit complaining about how stupid your colleagues are."

"But I am not trying to be liked. I am trying to get things done," she responded.

"Think of what you could accomplish if people actually wanted to help you," I replied.

I shared this story in the *Chronicle of Higher Education,* a publication for those who work in colleges and universities, and I was intrigued by the responses I received and the questions readers posed. It was clear that many readers struggled to know what it takes to be likable.

Smiling all the time? No. Sharing credit? Yes. Insincere compliments? No. Acknowledging colleagues when you pass them in the hall? Yes.

The comment-section banter was inadequate for some readers,

and a handful of them wrote to me directly (and bravely, I might add) admitting that they have struggled to be likable but were not entirely sure what they were supposed to do to connect with others. I think it is fair to say that likability is similar to art and pornography. We know it when we see it, but we are unlikely to reach uniform agreement on the concept. Still, the idea of a professional "likability list" seemed intriguing and prompted me to begin assembling one. Here are five attributes that make us seem likable:

Confidence balanced by humility

A friend of mine hosted a dinner party with several people I didn't know. As we were doing introductions, the first person up went on and on. After sharing his name, he reported on his many development projects, investment properties, local awards, and nonprofit board appointments. He concluded with "There's more, of course, but I don't want to go on all night. Ha, ha, ha."

The next guy, one of most respected space researchers in the United States, gave his name and said, "I'm in the University of Arizona Department of Astronomy."

Guy No. 1: Insecure? Overcompensating?
Definitely a blowhard = unlikable.

Guy No. 2: Quietly confident = immensely likable.

Making people feel valued / not making people feel stupid

The physician who had hired me to be his grants administrator early in my career was a skilled surgeon, a prolific researcher, and a man who had no patience for incompetence. During my early days on the job, I spent most of my time trying not to be a disappointment to him. One day, while he was being interviewed about male urologic cancers by our local radio station, a woman called in with a question that made me gasp: "We hear a lot about prostate cancer in men but much less about the disease in women. Why is that?" I held my breath, bracing for what I feared would be a biting and sarcastic response to this anatomy-challenged caller. After a brief pause, the surgeon delighted me with his charming response: "Other listeners might have the same question, so I'm glad you asked that. It's primarily because women don't have prostates. So, with women, we tend to hear more about breast, uterine, cervical, and ovarian cancers." I immediately fell in (work) love with him after that. Likable people know their stuff and have no need to make "lesser beings" feel inadequate.

Asking questions

Imagine attending a speed-dating event in which you have just a few minutes to speak with a partner before moving on to the next person. When you share your love of dogs with one speed-dating partner, she responds enthusiastically and shares a story about her beloved beagle, Peanut, who has a weird fondness for bananas. The story is funny, and you both laugh before moving to your next partner. You share your love of dogs with a second partner and have a very different experience. She mentions that she is currently without a dog and misses her golden retriever, Sandy, terribly. She asks how long you have had your dog, where you got him, and where you go on walks together. You spend so much time talking about your dog that you barely get to ask her any questions. At the end of the night, you are asked to make a list of people who you would like to see again. Who will get the offer? Peanut's owner, the great storyteller, or Sandy's former owner, who is currently dogless? Believe it or not, a research study like this was actually conducted. And guess what? The conversation partners who asked a lot of questions, including follow-up ones, received a significantly higher number of requests for second meetings. We are drawn to people who seem interested in us, and asking thoughtful questions increases our likability.[1]

But there is an art to asking questions. Author Stephen Covey once stated, "Most people do not listen with the intent to understand; they listen with the intent to reply."[2] It takes discipline to actually listen in a conversation, but focusing on the content and intentions of our conversation partner is essential for us to engage in meaningful dialogue. The more we pay attention, the more likable we become.

Speak other people's names

I have a colleague who uses my name all the time. "Hello, Allison." "Allison, that is a really good question." "I hadn't considered that, Allison, but I think you've got a point there." I am convinced that he is using my name very intentionally, but I don't care. I love to hear my name. And I bet he knows it.

Be real

While being vulnerable can be scary and painful, it is often the characteristic that makes us most likable and relatable. During a recent employment interview for a senior communications official, one candidate explained a gap in his work history with full honesty. "I recommended that my last employer elevate my communication role to a senior vice president position. My boss eventually agreed that he needed a senior vice president, but he also decided that it shouldn't be me. I had to think a lot about why he didn't think I was right for the role." In that moment, this candidate positioned himself as open, honest, and willing to admit to professionally stumbling. He won us all over immediately.

Being likable is an asset when attempting to navigate organizational politics or just survive in many environments. "Competent

Jerks, Lovable Fools, and the Formation of Social Networks" is one of my favorite research papers of all time. In it, Tiziana Casciaro and Miguel Sousa Lobo report the results of their study of for-profit and nonprofit organizations in the United States and Europe, which was designed to assess the value of likability.[3] They asked members of these organizations to indicate how often they had work-related interactions with everyone else in the organization. Next, they asked members to rate others based on how much they personally liked each one and how well their colleagues did their jobs.

Tiziana and Souso Lobo used these responses to the competence and likability questions to categorize organizational members as one of four archetypes: There is the competent jerk, who is proficient and knows a good deal but is unpleasant to deal with. The lovable fool is not talented but is fun to be around. The lovable star is both smart and likable, while the incompetent jerk makes no contributions and makes the workplace miserable.

While it is obvious that everyone wants to work with a lovable star and no one wants to work with an incompetent jerk, the researchers then asked managers whether they would prefer to work with a lovable fool or a competent jerk. The responses leaned heavily toward those with competence. Respondents suggested they could forgive jerks for their bad behavior as long as they were productive in some manner, but lovable fools were deemed rather useless. Yet when interaction patterns were analyzed, it turned out managers did the opposite of what they reported. In fact, they spent far more time with lovable fools than competent jerks, choosing to squeeze out any form of competence from the former and distancing themselves as far as possible from the latter. The lesson here? If you are not very smart, you had better be nice.

USE THE POWER OF SCARCITY

A representative from a local government organization contacted me with a speaking request. They imagined me delivering a spirited session titled "Delivering Compelling Presentations," and because the person who contacted me is a friend, it was clear she assumed I would happily agree. She seemed surprised when I responded, "I'm not the right person."

As she pressed me to reconsider, I resisted the urge to explain that being capable of designing a good presentation is one thing and wanting to do so is another. Instead, striving (as always) to demonstrate good manners, I explained that I only give talks on three general topics, and I invited her to consider whether one of those might fit her program. Polite. Firm. No openings for arguments. It felt good.

Having guardrails for evaluating options and opportunities was relatively new for me at the time, and being asked to speak to interesting groups felt highly validating. And then there was the guilt. Who was I to turn down a request from someone who needed me? I also thought about retribution and worried there would be consequences for declining, which happens to be a particularly gender-based phenomenon.[1] For too many years, I would hustle to meet external demands without attending to what made sense for *me*. I found myself exhausted and cranky and realized that being spread too thin wasn't serving anyone. The work

was draining rather than energizing, and I came to resent the people who asked for my time.

As I began struggling with how to handle unwanted requests, I started observing people who seemed to be doing better than me both professionally and personally. They appeared happier, lighter, and more optimistic. I noticed they all had something in common: they said "no" often and without any apparent angst.

I wondered if I should adopt the same approach. Would being more judicious with my time—and less likely to accept requests—make me a more serene person? I wrestled with that question because saying no seemed mean and ugly, while saying yes seemed gracious and generous. What to do? Looking for answers, I turned to the research on personal branding, where I learned that it was important to create a distinctive professional image and that it was better to be known for one thing or just a few related things than to be considered a utility player capable of filling multiple roles. [2] I also looked at the research on resource scarcity, and this is where I learned that declining invitations might make me more, rather than less, popular.

You already know that products and services that are difficult to acquire are perceived as more valuable than those that are more plentiful or accessible (think vintage cars, hard-to-secure reservations at a new restaurant, designer dresses, or autographed baseballs). It follows then that generally unavailable people are more in demand than those who readily accept any and all invitations. That is because we tend to covet what we cannot have or must wait for. In his paper "The Psychology of Unavailability: Explaining Scarcity and Cost Effects on Value," researcher Michael Lynn explains several of the psychological bases for our desire for things or people that are hard to acquire. [3] Lynn shares three truths that helped me understand that being constantly available is not good for our reputations or careers.

We love to be unique

Being able to secure a scarce resource signals that we are special in some way: "I have something special that you do not, and that makes me more special than you."

We crave recognition

The possession or display of a generally unavailable resource is a status symbol. "I have something few people have because I have something (money/connections/clout) that you do not."

We value quality

Lack of availability often signals that a resource is in high demand. When it comes to people, we assume that lack of availability is a function of being highly desirable to others. "It is hard to get on her consulting calendar because she is in such high demand by other clients."

Because the politically savvy often know how to use the power of scarcity to their advantage, they may cultivate an image of unavailability and practice some of the following techniques to make themselves seem important and in demand:

> **Scarcity strategy 1.** Rather than accepting a meeting that you have requested, your contact informs you that they will try to move things around to be available and then thanks you for your patience as they attempt to rearrange their calendar.

> **Scarcity strategy 2.** Instead of accepting the meeting date and time that you proposed based on information you were given regarding their availability, your contact's administrative assistant proposes an alternative date.

> **Scarcity strategy 3.** When asked to meet with a group for an

hour, your contact informs you that only the last thirty minutes will be possible.

Scarcity strategy 4. Rather than attend a gathering themselves, your contact asks if their participation is essential or whether they can send a designee.

The strategy of scarcity is also used to move others to action. Consider what happens when you go to book an airline flight at a preferred time and see "two tickets available at this price." The urgency you feel to scoop up the deal before others can make a purchase may drive you to pull out your credit card immediately rather than exploring other options. When you secure your spot, you may feel exceptionally satisfied to possess a seat that was clearly valuable to so many others.

The same tactics are often used to drive behavior in work and community settings. For example, as a strategy for making you feel special, a member of a prestigious nonprofit agency board informs you that while several people have expressed interest in joining the board, she wants to advance your name for the single seat available this year but needs to know your interest soon because other board members have favored candidates.

Is it ethical to create a false sense of scarcity to elevate your own status or to move others to action? I will leave that to you to determine, but the research on the power of scarcity should make you feel safe to decline invitations that are not aligned with your most strategic priorities. I eventually came up with my own formula for filtering requests, not to manipulate other people's perceptions of me but to give myself a decision framework for accepting or declining invitations. I no longer think about when to decline a request; instead, I think about what I need to say yes. Nowadays, I accept a request when one or more of the following is true:

- It is relatively easy to fulfill.
- It seems appropriately novel, fun, or energizing.
- It gives me an opportunity to highlight my strengths and professional expertise.
- Meeting the request would not significantly detract from other existing priorities.
- Doing so would fill a reservoir of goodwill I might need to draw upon later.
- It would expose me to new people who might be interesting or helpful.
- Tackling the challenge would enable me to learn something I had wanted to learn anyway.
- The recipients are likely to appreciate my time and effort.

If you are consistently overloaded and think defaulting to "yes" is the right political strategy, you can take some comfort in knowing that a regular use of "no" might actually get you more of what you want.

SAY "NO" GRACIOUSLY

Most all of us would agree that it makes sense to say no to people or activities that are not aligned with our most important priorities. Deciding to decline a request is the easy part. Delivering the news in a way that does not damage the way people think of us is a bit tougher. Because I struggle with disappointing others, I pay special attention to the artful ways the "thanks but no thanks" message can be delivered. I recently received a particularly good template for future use.

At a colleague's suggestion, I sent an email invitation to a well-regarded and high-profile expert I don't know very well. I wanted her to serve on an advisory committee and promised that we would be efficient, so the commitment would not be terribly burdensome. Two weeks went by without a word, so I assumed she had communicated her answer by not answering. And then something surprising happened. I got a response!

> *Allison, I've been trying to figure out a way to say that I could do this—because I would enjoy it. But the terrible truth is that I am really overcommitted in the next couple of years, and adding anything is probably not a good idea. I really hope I can help in the future.*

I am not so gullible as to think she was actually disappointed that she couldn't honor my request, but I appreciated the gracious and respectful way in which she responded. I decided immediately to add her approach to my repertoire

of ways to say no without sounding negative. Here are some other phrases that might work for you:

"I'm not the best person for that, so let me suggest [insert two names]."

"It would be so great to work with you on this, so I'm crushed that my schedule won't permit me to do this."

"I wish I could say yes, but I'm in the middle of a big project right now."

"This is an important event, and I'm afraid I wouldn't be able to give this the attention it deserves."

"Can you give me a few weeks to think about this and call you if I think I can make this work?"

"I wouldn't be able to participate on a regular basis but would be happy to serve as a sounding board from time to time."

"You are so kind to think of me. I wish I could."

We cannot make progress on our most strategic priorities if we are constantly diverted by requests from others, but we must balance the need for focus with the need to maintain valuable relationships. The way we decline requests sends an important message about who we are as people, and our goal should always be to make a requester feel honored even when we are turning them down. When making even a small a contribution is not possible, demonstrating graciousness is especially important.

KNOW WHEN TO SPEAK UP AND SHUT UP

A few days before a professional association conference in Tulsa, a person I admire contacted me to ask if we might have a serious conversation after we arrived at the conference hotel When I asked her what she wanted to discuss, she said she would let me know once we got together. We met in a bar, and I was curious to learn what she had to say. My colleague said she had been thinking about my prospects for securing a leadership role in the professional association and wanted to talk to me about behaviors that might limit my chances. "You talk a lot in meetings, and you interrupt constantly," she announced.

The description of my meeting behavior was painful news to hear, but it was delivered by a person I admired and trusted. In all honesty, it sounded a bit like some of the vague and less direct feedback I had been given in the past. So, despite being wounded, I expressed gratitude for the assessment and pledged to consider how I might change the way I interacted with others.

A couple of days later, with wounds just beginning to heal, I attended a committee meeting at work and said nothing—not just a little bit but nothing at all. While listening and nodding in all the right places, I uttered not one word. Finally, one of the people in attendance turned to me and asked, "What's happening here? Are you okay? You haven't said a word for thirty minutes." I explained that I was intentionally trying to talk less and listen more, and I was met with quizzical stares. "It doesn't seem normal for you to be so quiet," noted one of my colleagues.

That exchange came back to me during a recent meeting where all the usual suspects were doing plenty of talking, while a couple of people known for their strategic thinking remained silent. Knowing one of them to be incredibly shy, I felt it important to offer support and encouragement. As far as I am concerned, if you're not going to participate in a meeting, why bother to attend? I did not want this person to be regarded as wasting space.

I attempted an intervention through eyebrow messaging. I established eye contact and raised both eyebrows at once as if to signal, "Come on. Go for it. Please jump in here." This did not work. A few minutes later, I established eye contact again and employed a serious left-eyebrow-only raise complemented by an encouraging head twist. Still nothing. Feeling desperate, I increased my firepower by texting under the table, "You must say something today." As I pushed send, I noticed a message I had sent to the same recipient four months earlier in another setting: "You need to say at least one thing before the end of this meeting."

When my colleague finally spoke up to share an idea, the feedback was incredibly positive. "See? See?" I wanted to shout. "You are smart, and people actually like listening to what you have to say."

In reviewing my colleague's reticence to engage, I contrasted her behavior with a couple of colleagues who cannot keep quiet and consistently go on and on . . . seemingly forever and ever. They talk so much that when they open their mouths to speak, it almost serves as a cue for the rest of us to stop listening.

So what is the right formula for talking and not talking? Or, perhaps, what is the proper ratio of talking and listening intently? I'm not much for mathematical formulas, but if you are the one who captures most of the airtime in meetings, you are probably talking too much. And if you are perennially silent, you are sitting in a chair that would be better occupied by someone else.

Reluctant to express yourself? Try raising issues rather than making pronouncements. Asking a powerful question can be far more valuable than expressing a strong opinion. Better to be the one who ignites the conversation than the one who dominates it.

DEMONSTRATE THE POWER OF POISE

Call me paranoid or call me prepared, but I go through a ritual every time I'm scheduled to present at a conference.

Before leaving, I print out a copy of my slides in case all of my technology options fail. I then send copies of my presentation to two different email accounts and save versions onto two zip drives and one of my cloud accounts. Once I am onsite, I scope out the presentation venue immediately. When it is about time for the presentation to begin, I arrive early—always early—to make sure the technology works and to pour myself two glasses of water. Next, I attempt to forge connections with the people who arrive first to develop some early rapport and ferret out potential hecklers. I breathe deeply and remind myself that my audience wants me to succeed.

I went through that ritual during one conference and felt energized when the projector synched with the laptop without a hitch and a room with one hundred chairs quickly filled with more than one hundred people. *We are golden*, I thought to myself as my copresenter kicked off our session. If only.

The microphones that worked perfectly when the tech people were in the room failed to work at all once they disappeared, so after a bit of unsuccessful fiddling, my copresenter and I began to shout. Then, with horror, we watched a small brown bird that had apparently ingested cocaine zoom into our room and begin dive-bombing the scalps of people who

were tightly packed into the filled space. The bird traveled up and down, under chairs, up through people's legs, onto their shoulders, and into their necks—there were gasps and screams and squeals as the avian creature terrorized those held hostage in the room.

Chaos. Absolute chaos. And then, suddenly, it was quiet.

The bird, which was actually kind of cute in a maniacal kind of way, made its way to the front of the room and stood quietly on the floor next to me. Taunting me? I think so.

I needed to take action. Should I stomp on the bird's feather-covered head with my foot or try to stun it with the hard-copy version of my slides (maybe I was *meant* to print them!)? My mind raced, and my future passed before my eyes as I pictured people forever whispering, "She's the crazy one who killed that poor bird in Boston."

Plan B involved several failed attempts to trap the now-hopping bird with a sweater generously sacrificed by a colleague. Eventually, the adrenaline-crazed creature flew out of the room, over the head of the tech guy who had returned to fix our microphones. The presentation was saved.

Despite our best preparations, presentation disasters happen. The speaker who preceded you goes long, thereby requiring you to cram thirty minutes of content into fourteen. The session next door is loud, raucous, and full of laughter, prompting your audience to regret that they chose your session. You cannot, for the life of you, remember what you meant on slide eight. A know-it-all hijacks your session. You suddenly realize you have left the "i" out of the word "public" in your "Encouraging Public Discourse" title slide.

One of the most important aspects of professional presence is the ability to remain calm in the midst of calamity, and a mini-presentation crisis can actually be a way to engage your audience, create allies, and make yourself memorable. If you realize that you have misspelled a word on your slide, consider, "The next slide contains a typo. Raise your hand as soon as you spot it." If you forget what you meant on slide eight, simply move along while explaining, "In the interest of time, let me move to the next slide." If the technology fails and there is no way to present your information verbally, consider breaking up the audience into small groups and having them work on a problem together.

It can be helpful to remember that no one hopes the session they are attending will be terrible. They want it to be incredible. So if things go awry during your presentation, don't appear flustered or frustrated. Instead, dazzle your audience with your flexibility and good humor. This will position you as an unflappable pro and ensure that you are invited to speak again.

RESIST THE URGE TO EMBRACE YOUR FLAWS

Socrates, who took the phrase "know thyself" off a Greek temple and ran with it ("The unexamined life is not worth living"), might be disappointed to know that it has taken more than two thousand years for the importance of self-awareness to become a mainstream concept. But, finally, everyone seems to be talking about it—everyone in management positions, anyway. It is rare to have a conversation lately about workplace dynamics that does not include discussions about the notion of emotional intelligence and the critical need for self-awareness among those who want to effectively lead or interact with others.[1] Understanding our strengths, weaknesses, and blind spots is increasingly considered essential to good management.[2]

Daniel Goleman, a psychologist and author of the 1995 bestseller *Emotional Intelligence*, noted in an interview that self-aware leaders are more effective and productive: "What we used to think of as crises are now more routine, which means that it's more important for leaders to manage themselves as well as other people. It's about taking charge of a situation and not panicking."[3]

Supporting that perspective, Erich C. Dierdorff and Robert S. Rubin, both faculty members in management at DePaul University, wrote about self-awareness in a column for the *Harvard Business Review*. High levels of self-awareness, they argue, increase team performance, decision-making, and conflict management. They note, however, that

most of us are remarkably clueless about how others perceive us: "With no external data, the results of self-knowledge assessments are presumed to be accurate, when instead they may reinforce inaccurate perceptions of ourselves. The net result can be harmful to development and performance and, as we observed, the effectiveness of teams."[4]

That phenomenon is explored extensively in organizational psychologist Tasha Eurich's book *Insight*. According to Eurich, 85 percent of us have a faulty understanding of how we appear to others or how we affect them.[5] So, basically, almost all of us are clueless about how others perceive us. That is not good.

In an effort to improve those numbers, many organizations offer current and emerging leaders the opportunity to increase awareness of the strengths moving them forward and the challenges holding them back. Peer coaching is one strategy. One-on-one management or executive coaching is another. More common are assessments called 360 reviews, which invite a mix of colleagues and even customers or clients to offer their perspectives via a survey tool that assesses various leadership competencies. In addition to asking survey respondents to offer ratings on different leadership attributes, many 360-degree feedback surveys include open text boxes that ask what the employee should start doing, stop doing, do more of, or do less of to be more effective.

You would think all of this honesty would be paying big dividends. But I have noticed a surprising trend: I see more and more leaders who seem to be embracing negative feedback and almost bragging about their perceived deficits while continuing to engage in the very behaviors that colleagues have asked them to stop or tone down—things like:

"I know people think I have too much to say," shared one person who tends to go on and on—while, of course, going on and on and on.

"Apparently, people consider me dismissive, but that's just their opinion," another leader recently explained as she proceeded to reject the perspectives of everyone around the table who disagreed with her.

One leader who is known for overcommitting and underdelivering commented, "I know I tend to overcommit, but that's just who I am. I think most people understand that when I say yes, my intentions are good."

Yet another commented, "People say I'm brusque. I can see that, but I am unusually efficient, and I think that is more important."

I'm curious: when did it become acceptable to embrace the characteristics that others have identified as detrimental to our mutual professional success?

I suspect many of the people who trot out their fatal flaws are attempting to create a defense shield to protect themselves from further criticism: "You will not speak of my fatal flaws because I have mentioned them first and am therefore immune to your potential condemnation." It's a classic offense-as-defense strategy.

That approach may work for a while, but eventually it prompts some pointed questions:

"If you know you talk too much, why do you continue to take up all the airtime?"

"If you know you are considered dismissive, why do you believe it is in your best interest to denounce the perspectives of anyone who thinks differently than you do?"

"If you know you overpromise and underdeliver, what makes you think people will continue to take you seriously?"

"Why do you assume steamrolling over others is a sustainable strategy?"

It is good to be self-aware. But demonstrating self-awareness while at the same time showing a lack of discipline to fix issues of concern is worse than being clueless about our shortcomings. When people close to us offer consistent and considerable feedback about a behavior that is not serving us well, we need to listen up. Dismissing feedback that does not comport with the way we see ourselves is understandable, but it is not strategic. The most effective people I know sometimes whimper for a bit after receiving constructive criticism, but they quickly put a plan in place to modify the annoying or offending behaviors. By doing so, they demonstrate respect and appreciation for those brave enough to share difficult truths that are offered with the very best intentions. We need our colleagues to help us be better, but they can't help if we're not listening. When we fail to acknowledge or act upon feedback offered with honesty and the best of intentions, we signal that we are not truly open to the feedback we have requested. Eventually, we will cease to receive the guidance or even the warnings we need.

AVOID SHINING
TOO BRIGHTLY

Have you recently been recognized for landing a prized sales account? Received attention for completing a project on time and under budget? Been promoted to a coveted role? Finally secured an appointment to a high-profile committee? Garnered attention for your specialized expertise? While you might expect your friends and colleagues to celebrate your success, their applause might well be tempered by expressions of envy that could ultimately compromise your career. Whenever you are tempted to bask in the limelight, be sure you are simultaneously watching your back, for it is when we are at the top of our game that we may face the most peril.

History offers an important life lesson about the dangers that come with doing well. You may be familiar with what happened centuries ago when the son of Roman king Lucius Tarquinius Superbus needed some advice about how to manage his political opponents. Rather than visiting his father to obtain the guidance he needed, the son sent a messenger to his father's residence to ask what he should do with those who might challenge his power. After greeting the messenger and hearing his son's question, the king did not provide a written or verbal response. Instead, he ventured into his garden and picked up a stick. Without uttering a word, the king meandered throughout the garden, whacking the tops off the tallest poppies.

The messenger, frustrated that the king was refusing to provide the requested advice, returned to the city of Gabii and told the king's son what he had seen. The son realized his father had actually answered his inquiry with great precision. His father was instructing him to lop off the heads of his own tallest poppies—the most powerful people of Gabii. So the younger Sextus proceeded to kill them all. Historians point to this story as the basis for the term "tall poppy," which is often used to describe a person whose conspicuous success attracts envy and hostility.[1]

Several researchers, among them Eugene Kim and Theresa M. Glomb, have found that instead of being able to celebrate their success, high performers often find themselves targets of victimization by coworkers who are envious of their success or worried that their high performance will raise expectations for others in the group. In their cleverly titled article "Get Smarty Pants: Cognitive Ability, Personality, and Victimization," Kim and Glomb report that those with high cognitive abilities—smart people—are particularly at risk of being victimized by others.[2] We knew the smart kids were bullied in junior high, but apparently picking on high performers never truly goes out of style.

While most of us would never actually kill the tall poppies among us, we can be remarkably creative when it comes to bringing them back into line. The options seem almost limitless and can include shunning, withholding information, offering effusive and insincere public praise that is followed by snarky condemnation in private, and even alleging the decision-making that elevated our target was rigged in some manner. We work especially hard to make sure that those we consider arrogant or undeserving don't shine too brightly for too long.

So what should we do if our accomplishments garner significant attention or result in our getting what others may have wanted?

How can we protect ourselves from those who may experience anger or envy? Certainly, demonstrating a good amount of humility is a good strategy, as is downplaying accomplishments, but we should be aware that false modesty can often look insincere. Honestly sharing the challenges, struggles, and setbacks we faced along the road to success can be especially effective, as creating a sense of "deservingness" seems to reduce the likelihood that we will be taken down by others.[3] Success born of struggle seems to be more acceptable than success that emerges without great effort or sacrifice.

Focusing on our colleagues rather than ourselves—engaging in what is called organizational citizenship behavior—can be an especially smart strategy. Supporting the success of others can create a certain amount of goodwill and interdependence, and shifting the spotlight from ourselves to our workgroups can be a powerful source of protection. When team members view our high performance as contributing to their own success by making it possible to accomplish difficult tasks, elevating their status, or securing additional resources, they are less likely to engage in professional victimization.[4] Creating a sense of connection with colleagues can be a protective strategy as well because otherness often gives colleagues moral license to abuse us. It is easier to mistreat those who seem different. When we distance ourselves, through isolation or by suggesting we are superior, we may be at special risk for a painful career takedown. Put concisely, we should be kind and helpful if we want to be safe.

If you have not achieved tall poppy status yet but are well on your way, have you considered that your decapitation could be imminent? It is wise to plan for your success before you achieve it. The way you handle your newfound status may well determine whether your head metaphorically stays on your shoulders or is intentionally lopped off.

GETTING AHEAD

STRIVE TO BE NOTICED

During an awards ceremony I attended, a truly remarkable recipient was described as strong, silent, and too focused on his work to seek recognition. That is not how award winners are generally described because the people who tend to receive acclaim are those who actively seek attention and acknowledgment for their contributions. They may apply for awards themselves or encourage colleagues to submit nominations on their behalf. There are many paths to high-visibility recognition, but working diligently and hoping to be noticed is not typically a winning strategy. The realization that we need to be strategic about ensuring that our contributions are recognized can be a hard and frustrating truth for those who believe that good work speaks for itself and shy away from self-promotion.

Getting ahead professionally tends to be easier when one is recognized and well regarded. Evaluations are higher, nominations for positions and awards come more easily, invitations to speak or serve on high-profile project teams occur more frequently, and referrals for consulting or advice are more likely. Being visible and connected also increases job security as it is harder to oust people who have a solid base of support. There is really no question that a strong presence and reputation make new opportunities easier to identify and pursue. But how do we create personal buzz for ourselves? What is the best way to build a solid reputation? How can we increase our visibility without being tiresome?

I have learned a lot about the right ways and wrong ways to publicize accomplishments from two colleagues

who are extraordinarily talented and highly visible. While both are recognized for their drive, intelligence, and expertise, people tend to find one of them charming and the other one insufferable. What accounts for the difference? It is really pretty simple. One promotes ideas, while the other promotes herself. One shares information, and the other shares what can only be characterized as personal press releases. One celebrates the accomplishments of her colleagues, while the other thanks her colleagues for making her success possible. One is always mentioned as someone people want on their committees or project teams, and the other prompts eye-rolling and sighing each time her name is mentioned.

If the old adage about good work speaking for itself was ever true, it is certainly not true these days. That's why maintaining a professional edge means being intentional about cultivating professional visibility and ensuring that good work is recognized. The key is to generate regular visibility without seeming like a braggart or blowhard. So what is the best way to increase visibility without being perceived as a shameless self-promoter? Here are a few strategies to consider:

- *First, do no harm.* The goal is to have people talk about you—in a good way. You can be perfectly brilliant, but if people talk trash about you, you'll achieve the wrong kind of visibility. You probably have your own list of behaviors that lead to negative visibility, and I'll admit to talking about people who are chronically late to meetings, cancel commitments at the last minute, hog airtime, pontificate, spout uninformed conspiracy theories, make people cry, steal credit from others, and yammer on about their many accomplishments. Be the person whom others admire and want to succeed.

- *Help others be successful.* When we praise others publicly or go out of our way to help remove a barrier or solve a problem, our colleagues will often be inspired to return the favor and seek to elevate us in some way.

- *Create visibility for yourself by promoting the achievements of others.* Speaking up in a meeting to congratulate a coworker for the successful completion of a project or solving a vexing technical problem goal shines the spotlight on you in a positive manner. Highlighting the work or achievements of a friend or colleague using social media can be equally effective. Being visible doesn't require talking about yourself; elevating others is often a much better strategy.

- *Be focused.* I know many people find calls for personal branding to be annoying, but doing this work truly matters. It may make you feel better to focus on creating a professional niche. Regardless of what we call it, it's important to think about the mental image we want others to have about us. A sense of consistency is important, so think about how you want people to consider your work and your style. Take a little time to write down three phrases that capture who you are or who you want to be and make sure that your behaviors, actions, and decisions are consistently aligned with those descriptors. Want to be considered edgy, innovative, and future-oriented? Think about the podcasts you discuss, the ideas you advance, and even the clothes you wear. Want to convey a serious and disciplined vibe? Make sure you leave the bar before others and are known for taking a run before your first cup of coffee. People are watching.

- *Share your ideas as much as possible.* Debating whether you really have time to make a presentation at a local nonprofit meeting or share your work at an internal planning retreat? Unless you are likely to embarrass yourself by being unprepared, seize every opportunity to share your ideas and work.

- *Offer ideas and valuable content for free.* Sharing useful information, providing free templates or assessment tools, and forwarding articles that might be helpful to others are just a few ways we can increase our personal visibility in a way that does not seem like we are intentionally seeking attention. Being a curator takes much less time than being a creator but yields similar dividends.

- *Offer to speak without a fee.* Professional associations, community groups, and nonprofit organizations are venues for sharing your expertise and increasing your visibility.

- *Include your latest successes at the bottom of every meeting agenda with your boss.* You don't even need to speak of the successes; just make a routine of reminding your boss about your achievements. Attaching invitation letters or expressions of appreciation offers useful evidence that you are being recognized by others.

- *Be appropriately visible but not perpetually available.* I received this advice many years ago and have to admit to struggling with it a bit. If people ask me to attend something, I tend to want to be accommodating. However, a mentor once told me that I suffer from terminal niceness. "Being too accessible also diminishes people's perception of your value. You need to go to things that will advance *your* agenda, not *their* agenda, and that means saying no even when there is time on your calendar."

- *Let others promote you.* Did you win an award? Have you published an article that might have popular appeal? Were you appointed to a professional association or community leadership position? Make sure an announcement gets forwarded to your communication office. Having your organization or local press publicize your accomplishments looks better than spouting off about yourself, but don't be afraid to announce your good news on your own social media sites. Getting a friend or colleague to share your good news with others can be especially powerful as well. If you get into the habit of doing it for them, they will do it for you.

- *Provide just-in-time, specialized expertise.* Rather than signing on for a time-consuming team or project, offer to provide expertise that no one else possesses when the time is right. Excellent at creating captivating presentations? Build a template for the team to fill in. Are you an expert at conducting statistical analysis? Offer to make sense of survey responses. Know someone who might be willing to open their home for a political candidate house party? Make the introduction and be on hand for the event. Filling an urgent need can often generate more gratitude and visibility than being a general committee member.

- *Create a reciprocity ring.* A reciprocity ring is formed when two or more people commit to help each other, and this may include cross-promoting one another.[1] One person may want help getting recommended for high-profile projects. Another may want to be nominated for a professional award. A member of your reciprocity ring may want to be suggested as a member of a prestigious nonprofit board, while another might be seeking a new job and would benefit from a personal introduction to the hiring manager.

To some people, these suggestions seem overly calculating and even unethical, but they are not. They are strategic. If you look closely at those who are highly visible, you will likely find that they achieved their prominence by being thoughtful and deliberate about cultivating a professional persona. They know that to advance an idea, secure support for a cause, or get ahead professionally, they need to be noticed—and so do you.

PRACTICE PARTY TIPS FOR INTROVERTS

It is politically important to see and be seen, and attending parties and special events is a good way to renew connections, meet potential collaborators, and increase your professional visibility. But what if the social scene is difficult for you because you are shy or your introverted nature makes working a party mentally exhausting? What if you know that it is socially and politically important to be visible at gatherings but would much rather stay home? If that describes you, know that you are not alone. In her book *Quiet: The Power of Introverts in a World That Can't Stop Talking*, Susan Cain reports that between one-third and half of all people are drained by crowded social situations.[1]

If you find business and social gatherings mentally exhausting to navigate, having a game plan before reaching the event can be helpful. Here are a few moves for you to consider.

In advance, ask the event host if you can help with setup or serving. "Working" the party can give you something important to do and an opportunity to interact with others in a natural way. Volunteer to serve as the official photographer, bartender, or snack passer.

Arrive just as the event begins. Your host will not be distracted by others and will be in a position to assign you a last-minute job such as cutting up limes for the margaritas. Your host will also be in a better position to introduce you to guests as they arrive. It can actually feel less awkward to

be the first person to show up than to arrive once a gathering is in full gear.

Whenever possible, take a plus-one.[2] That person can be a friend or a colleague who might benefit from some new connections. Having a party partner can be a tremendous source of support.

Inquire about the guest list in advance and make it your mission to introduce yourself to at least two people who seem interesting before the gathering. It's easy. "I'm [your name], and I have always wanted to meet you." Who could be put off by that? Better yet, contact these people in advance to let them know you will be looking for them.

Be prepared with a compelling twenty- to thirty-second response to "What's new with you?"

Stand by the bookshelf and discuss your host's reading tastes with those around you.[3]

Try walking outside; there, you will often find a fellow introvert trying to decompress from people overload.

Hang out in the kitchen and just listen to everyone else talk.

Come armed with something interesting to talk about. See a movie or attend a street festival before the event so you can talk about what you were just doing.

Do a little extra reading, check out a new TV show, or listen to a few podcasts in the days leading up to the event so you can drop a fun fact. I remember when the news hit about it no longer being advisable to wash chicken before cooking it. The counterintuitive salmonella story carried me for several weeks.

Seek out those who appear to be the life of the party. Big talkers like good listeners.[4] If you give them your full attention, you will be under no obligation to talk yourself, not that you would be able to even if you tried.

Wear something interesting that can serve as a conversation starter.[5] "Thanks. I have a collection of ties inspired by artwork. You probably recognize this as *The Scream* by Edvard Munch. Are you an art fan?" Or, "Yes, I made these earrings myself. Making jewelry is one of my favorite hobbies. What do you do in your free time?"

Memorize some conversation starters:

"How do you know the host?"

"What is your connection to this organization?"

"What was the best thing you did this summer?"

"Any big holiday plans?"

"Do you know a lot of the people here?"

"What are you most excited about these days?"

"What's happening at work this year?"

"What would a perfect weekend be for you?"

"I'm looking for a new TV show. Any recommendations?"

"Have you tried any good restaurants lately?"

What should you do if you are stuck in a conversation that is draining you? Invite someone else in to join the discussion and then say, "I'm going to check out the appetizers; would you like me to bring something back for you?" Or, even better, "Oh, I see my friend Chen. I will be right back."

While it may be tempting to avoid social engagements, being seen in settings outside of work offers you a sense of social proof: "If she knows the host, she must have more connections than I imagined," or "He's deep in conversation with the head of strategy; he must be more interesting than I gave him credit for." You do not need to stay for long, but it is almost always better to accept an invitation than to decline one.

Social gatherings can also be fortuitous spots for making progress on a key project at work: "You didn't seem convinced about opening an office in Vancouver during the strategy meeting last week. I am interested to know more about your perspectives on that." Being able to secure more information in a casual setting can give you an edge that will strengthen your position when you are back in the office.

Still feeling anxious about attending a gathering where you might not know a lot of people? Remember that the event will be easier to navigate with a bit of advance preparation, an interesting outfit or accessory, and a willingness to carry used plates and glasses back to the kitchen. If attending someone else's event seems painful, take a lesson from marketing and strategy consultant Dorie Clark and create your own party.[6] Everyone will be delighted to be invited, and you can populate your gathering with people you actually like or have always wanted to get to know.

BUILD YOURSELF
A BRAIN TRUST

The work I do puts me in regular contact with people who are intelligent, articulate, poised, and deeply engaged in their work. Given their obvious talents and insights, I am regularly surprised that so many of them struggle to make sense of the organizational politics that drive decision-making in the worlds in which they exist. They often make up complicated stories to explain the allocation of promotions and resources or assume that sinister motives are driving the bulk of key decisions. Their conjecture is fascinating, but it is usually wrong.

Those who are consistently off base about the real drivers of organizational activity generally have one thing in common: they lack a broad and diverse network of colleagues and advisors. They may have plenty of friends and colleagues, but when these friends and colleagues travel in the same circles, they often lack true insights about organizational priorities. Without data and guidance to make sense of the world around them, these individuals connect dots that should remain unconnected and make up stories to explain various situations.

So how do we position ourselves to be more informed about organizational dynamics and better able to gather useful intelligence? Many of us are advised to secure a strategic and high-powered mentor. While that can be a useful strategy for improving skills, receiving encouragement, or

obtaining advice, establishing a brain trust is likely to be a more valuable strategy.

So what is a brain trust? The moniker is said to have surfaced during Franklin Roosevelt's presidency when Roosevelt's speechwriter and legal counsel, Samuel Rosenman, urged him to assemble an academic team to advise him on many of the intractable issues facing the United States. Roosevelt accepted the advice and set about to recruit three Columbia University law professors to offer him strategic guidance. Observing the work of Adolf A. Berle, Raymond Moley, and Rexford Guy Tugwell, *New York Times* reporter James M. Kieran dubbed the group Roosevelt's "Brain Trust."[1] These men, and others who eventually joined them, played a key role in shaping the policies of the First New Deal in the early 1930s.

Like Roosevelt, almost all of us could benefit from a dedicated brain trust that serves as a personal board of advisors ready to offer us advice, help us wrestle with ethical dilemmas, interpret events, share perspectives on our current challenges, critique our decisions, and position us to move forward with greater confidence. But do you need a group of Columbia University professors to help you with your career? Of course not. You simply need a collection of people who want you to be successful and are willing to provide you with guidance and insights from time to time. You do not need to hold formal meetings or publish a membership roster. It is not even necessary to ask for formal participation. The group forms a collective in your life, not in all of theirs. A simple "I really appreciate the way you think; would you be willing to let me run ideas by you from time to time?" can be a low-key way of establishing your relationship as something official.

The mechanics of establishing a personal board of advisors are not that hard to master. The tougher challenge is deciding on the membership. There is no template that works for everyone as we all need a different mix of people. Here are a few archetypes that might prove helpful to you:

The packager can make even a small idea seem like a well-established national model by creating a tagline, a website, or an active social media presence. Look to this person to help you create excitement about an idea or convince others that a current project has widespread visibility.

The political strategist sees life as a series of chess moves. She may work with real-life politicians every day or be an internal organizational strategist who can help you see the potential ramifications of your ideas and proposed approaches. Look to her when weighing politically charged and high-stakes options.

The insider is close to those who hold formal and informal power. This individual knows and sees all and serves as an important translator of decisions and resource allocations. The insider usually knows who is connected to whom and can alert us to unwritten rules. Want to know the best time to introduce a new idea or which font is particularly annoying to a decision maker? The insider will know.

The pop culture expert can be your go-to source for the latest in memes, movies, TV trends, podcasts, and celebrity news that can be incorporated into cocktail party conversations, writing, and presentations. Spending time with the pop culture expert will make you seem well read, worldly, and remarkably on top of emerging trends.

The mediator understands people and can help us resolve conflict. Fighting with a coworker or struggling to make sense of why you might have upset a key influencer? The mediator can offer a systematic guide to minimizing the conflict by suggesting listening, negotiation, and collaboration strategies.

The technologist will keep you up to date on software programs and emerging technologies. When you can speak with confidence about new enterprise systems, cybersecurity threats, or newly released project management tools, you will seem strategic and informed.

The industry scanner is adept at noticing trends in your field before anyone else is. This person can help you suggest bold and future-oriented ideas.

The fashionista always looks pulled together and offers advice on everything from eyebrow trends to proper tie widths.

The social media expert can teach you how to use various platforms to manage your digital presence.

The business guru has deep expertise in corporate life and can be a go-to source on ethical dilemmas, start-up cultures, and board dynamics.

The connector knows everyone in your community and is always willing to make an introduction. Because connectors seem to know and hear all, they can offer early-warning alerts. Your connector is likely to share, "Two software companies are merging, and the new entity is going to handle all marketing in-house" or "The city's biggest corporate real estate firm called recently to ask for leads on a senior director for business development candidate."

The career advisor is a career coach or search firm consultant who knows how to tell a story with a résumé and can give you wise advice about how to navigate an interview.

The entrepreneur runs a business and knows how to hustle. The entrepreneur will often tell you that you are spending too much time on things that do not make an impact. Listen when you are offered that advice.

The Zen master has an established mindfulness practice and keen sense of discipline. Pay attention when the Zen master tells you that you can afford fifteen minutes of meditation each morning and suggests you buy a good-quality reflection journal to scribble the chaos out of your head each night.

The truth teller will tell you what you need to know, knowing that you would prefer not to know it. The truth teller can identify strengths while at the same time pointing out opportunities for development.

There are other archetypes, of course, but perhaps these examples will help you imagine the kinds of people you might want on your personal board of advisors. The more diverse your brain trust, the better, so if all members look alike, come from the same backgrounds, or share similar beliefs, you will not receive the diversity of thought, perspective, and experience you need to make informed decisions. When it comes to building a brain trust, it is best to strive for eclecticism rather than comfort.

KEEP YOUR AMBITION IN CHECK

Plenty of people find ambition to be distasteful, but I am not one of them. Want a bigger role, a fancier title, more money, an opportunity to make a bigger impact? I say, "Go for it." But until you land that next opportunity, remember: you still need to attend to the job you have now. And that is precisely where I see the careers of many ambitious people start to fall apart. In my years working with and in various organizations, I have seen people at all levels get so fixated on moving up that they ignore both their current assignments and the colleagues who have supported their success. Rather than continuing to hustle to do well in the job they have, they put all their energy into landing the one they want.

Those of you who follow US politics may recall what happened to the career of former New Jersey governor Chris Christie, who expected to parlay his role at the state level into one on the national stage. During the weeks leading up to his departure from elected office, there was a lot of chatter about why there was no obvious next step for Christie, despite his significant name recognition. Several political pundits suggested that his performance as governor was hampered by his pursuit of a larger national role.[1] Many argued he was so busy trying to make a name for himself that he neglected the office he was elected to run.[2] He was widely viewed as a man who was out for himself. But should we fault Governor Christie for wanting to play on a national stage? I don't think so. He might have enjoyed more success, however, had he

paid more attention to the people at home while making his case for something bigger.

I see a distinct difference between ethically oriented high achievers and those who are unscrupulously ambitious. Both types want to move up the ladder, but people in the first group concentrate on making their organizations or communities better, while those in the latter group focus on making things better for themselves. Ethical high achievers attend to their responsibilities while pursuing bigger roles, while the unscrupulously ambitious tend to ignore their current jobs—or shift their work to others—to create more time for pursuing the next big thing.

The unscrupulously ambitious tend to be predictable, which makes me wonder if there is a *Slacker's Field Guide to Getting Ahead at All Costs* out there that I have yet to discover. If such a book exists, I imagine that it includes the following strategies:

- Sign on to lead high-profile projects and then appoint a trusted deputy to do all the work while you make all the public presentations.

- Suddenly develop a provocative point of view, sense of outrage, or deep concern about the state of your industry that is expressed by writing articles and opinion pieces that call for action—without actually doing anything about those issues under your control.

- Volunteer to take on a department no one wants or tackle a problem that no one else wants to handle. Once this item is documented on your résumé, foist it upon someone else, claiming that they are the more appropriate owner.

- Whenever possible, seek opportunities to present to your board of directors or trustees or testify in front of city officials, state legislators, or members of Congress—because visibility matters.

- Make sure people on your internal communications team

are aware of your every move. Demand that they write flattering stories about your new initiatives and issue press releases whenever you win an award.

- Insist on being at the microphone, or close to it, whenever there are positive announcements to make in your organization and intentionally distance yourself from negative news to ensure that your name only comes up in internet searches when the context is positive.

- Pursue leadership roles on commissions, professional organizations, and high-status nonprofit boards that will not require you to do any actual work.

- While citing the need to support better organizational alignment, make a move to shift as many people and departments as possible under your box on the organizational chart. More is always better.

- If a well-regarded member of your team announces plans to leave for a larger role in a better organization, take credit for launching their career. If the departure is clearly designed to escape from your leadership, whisper to the grapevine that you asked that person to leave. Remember, good people never leave *you*.

It takes an impressive portfolio and track record to rise above all the other stars who are competing for bigger roles too. The unscrupulously ambitious know that, which is why they often resort to a lot of intense résumé-building behavior around the time they are deciding to make a move. But that kind of last-minute achievement stacking can backfire when it leads those up and down the organizational chart to feel used, played, or ignored.

Support and respect from one's colleagues are hard to quantify on a résumé, but those are the qualifications that so often make or break a candidacy. We earn that support and respect by making our current organization stronger, honoring our commitments, and taking good care of the people who take care of us. When our hunger for the next big thing prompts us to trample over others or take credit for work without actually doing it, we may find ourselves much like Chris Christie—without the job we want and out of the job we had.

DON'T CURB YOUR ENTHUSIASM

The path from job applicant to potential finalist can be a bumpy journey, and it can be hard to know how to act at each step of the process. Early in my career, I was coached to act cool and almost uninterested when informed that I was moving to the next step of the hiring process. "People want what they can't have, so make them fight for you," I was advised. Once I moved to the other side of the hiring table and had the power to make job offers, I found this cavalier sense of coolness annoying when demonstrated by candidates. Their ambivalence and apparent lack of enthusiasm made them less desirable, not more, and I learned to turn my attention to candidates who were excited about an opportunity and not afraid to admit it.

There are many ways to express enthusiasm, and one of the best I've seen occurred in a candidate's job talk, a presentation in which a candidate describes their vision for the role and then takes questions from those in attendance. In one of these sessions in a university setting, a candidate concluded her "vision for the future" presentation with a highly scripted closing. "I've been doing a lot of research on the search process and even talking with search firms about what differentiates successful and unsuccessful candidates," she explained. "Through this, I've come to appreciate that organizations often worry that candidates aren't sufficiently excited about the opportunity. Well, I want you to know that I really want this job." The final presentation slide was then advanced, and the screen showed a photo of the candidate holding a sign that read "I really want to be your next dean of students." This candidate's presentation got attention because it is so unusual for candidates to express such obvious enthusiasm. In addition to believing that playing hard to get is a smart move, many candidates demonstrate an "I could take it or leave it" attitude because they subscribe to one or more of the following beliefs:

"Expressing enthusiasm will make me look desperate."

Actually, expressing enthusiasm will make you look, well, enthusiastic. Of course, it takes a little timing to pull this off. Too much enthusiasm too early can make you look naïve. It's best to start by appearing intensely curious and pleased to be considered. Once you know enough to be genuinely committed to pursuing a job, expressing enthusiasm will signal excitement about both the opportunity and the people with whom you would work. The people responsible for hiring and potential new colleagues gravitate toward those who seem energized about coming aboard. Convince them that you would feel honored to be selected.

"Appearing to want a position will weaken my negotiating position."

In my experience, negotiations go better when the hiring authority and the candidate are equally excited about the opportunity to make a match. Savvy candidates and smart hiring authorities position the negotiation process as a problem-solving exercise rather than a protracted wrestling match over resources. Candidates say, "I really want to be here and will just need X, Y, and Z to make that happen." Hiring authorities respond, "How can we remove the barriers that are keeping us from sealing this deal?" When both parties are excited, more possibilities are created.

"If I don't get the job, it will be less embarrassing to have acted like I didn't care."

None of us likes to be rejected, so it can be tempting to act as if we don't care in order to protect our psyches in the event we are not selected. Search committees and managers tend to pick up on this aloofness and read it as lack of interest and commitment. Being open about what we want might make us a bit vulnerable, but it doesn't make us losers. When we are honest about what we want, we make it easier for people to give it to us.

When hiring committees and decision makers are conducting their final analyses, which of the finalists seems to want the job most is often factored into the decision. I have been in multiple conversations in which the committees debated how happy the candidate would be if the job were offered and how long it would be before another time-consuming search would be required to fill the role when the candidate got bored or frustrated. These conversations occur far less often when the finalist expresses appreciation for the position in question, the culture of the organization, and the community where the role exists.

If you truly want the job you are interviewing for, be bold. Declare your desire for the role and express excitement and enthusiasm. This will make you more competitive, not less desirable.

ACCEPT INTERIM ROLES WITH CAUTION

At a recent conference, I caught up with a colleague and learned that his organization, like so many lately, had welcomed a new leader who was in the process of replacing several people on the team he inherited. Given my friend's well-known "good citizen" status, he had been recommended as a trustworthy placeholder for one of these roles while a search firm worked its magic to find a more permanent placement. "I think I want to do this," he said to me, "but I wonder if accepting this interim assignment might actually hurt my career in the long run."

The opportunity to hold a major leadership role, even temporarily, seemed validating and intellectually invigorating, he said. He imagined fixing things that needed to be fixed and even positioning himself to be competitive for the real job. At the same time, he knew of at least one faction of people who would attempt to sabotage him for accepting a position that they had expected would go to the ousted leader's second-in-command. My colleague wondered aloud about several questions. Would the interim assignment serve as an opportunity for professional growth? Or would it be the first step in unraveling all of the goodwill he had built over several years? Would the assignment make him stronger and more marketable? Or would he emerge irrevocably bruised from internal political squabbles?

My colleague was smart to be asking such questions because those who have served in interim roles know that these assignments have the potential to either elevate or sink careers. An interim appointment can be a remarkable leadership-development opportunity. It can allow time to explore the complexities of a senior leadership role and even cement the perception that you are capable of handling bigger challenges. There are risks, however. If you fumble in the position, you can create doubt about your ability to take on more responsibility and even generate concern about whether you are suited to return to the role you held before.

If you are approached about accepting an interim assignment, you might find it helpful to consider the following questions.

Why am I being asked to serve in this capacity?

If you are offered an interim role rather than having applied for one, it is wise to ask why your name surfaced. Was your name put forth because of your leadership potential, because your boss wants you to play a slash-and-burn role, or because you are someone who can be counted on to keep the trains running on time without any change or drama? Is it possible you have been offered the role because you are sure to fail, which will better position someone else to swoop in and look like a star? In short, are you considered a contender, a disrupter, a caretaker, or a sucker? Once you know what is expected, you can decide whether you want to play that role.

What is the process for making this interim appointment?

As a big believer in a fair and open hiring process, I regularly advise leaders to issue a call for expressions of interest and nominations for an interim position. You never know who might come forward. Furthermore, going through a formal review process generally provides a sense of legitimacy that enhances the interim appointee's credibility and success. While it is tempting for an organization to name an interim leader without any form of competition, if you are chosen under those circumstances, be prepared for political backlash and additional scrutiny.

Can I be considered for the real role if I decide I am interested?

Some organizations make it a practice to exclude interims from consideration for permanent roles. The reasons include a belief that this restriction reduces "campaigning" by those in the interim role. But I have seen several interims accept a role for which they had no long-term interest only to find that they actually enjoyed the work. I have also seen interims accept a role with trepidation and then discover they were highly effective. In both cases, there was a fair amount of disappointment when they were denied the opportunity to compete in the search process. Think seriously about whether to accept the interim role if it means you are prohibited from pursuing the real position.

Can I jump in, or will I be expected to hang back?

If you are going to accept an interim role, be sure you will be allowed to go all in. If you are instructed not to make waves or in any way demonstrate true leadership, consider declining the role. Why? Because no one admires a caretaker. You can claim that you were told not to make any big decisions, but few people will believe you. Instead, they will assume you lacked the vision or energy to make things happen. When a real role emerges, you will be marked as the one who didn't really do anything when you had the chance.

How long will the assignment last?

Interim appointments give organizations an opportunity to breathe: "We've got someone in place, so we can take our time to find the right person." While these posts can offer career-development opportunities and even a temporary increase in pay, interim appointees often feel abused once the excitement of the new role wears off—especially if they want the real position but all the signs indicate that is not going to happen. Before accepting an interim assignment, find out when it is expected to end or at least ask for a check-in date. If, by that date, the assignment needs to be extended and you are feeling abused, ask for something—travel money to be used later, new laptops for the people in your home department, a minisabbatical, even a spot on a high-profile project. You want to feel good about this opportunity, not burdened and misused by it.

Will I be expected to do this job in addition to my regular role?

Taking on an interim gig while being expected to serve effectively in your regular post is often a sure way to fail at both. When possible, negotiate the temporary distribution of your current responsibilities to someone else, thereby giving one or more people the opportunity to join you in growing professionally.

Will I be taken seriously?

Candidates selected after a rigorous review process are generally considered to be legitimate victors, but interim appointees often struggle to be taken seriously. If the interim assignment is aligned with your current work and responsibilities, you should be fine. If the role seems to be well beyond your wheelhouse, prepare to be challenged at every step.

What will I gain from this role?

It might be new connections, greater visibility, opportunities to advance new ideas, or experience managing a large group of people. Think about what you want to gain and achieve from an interim assignment and take deliberate steps to pursue those things. Ensure that you will grow in the role.

How will I make my mark?

An interim appointment is an item you can add to your résumé, whether or not you decide to pursue the real role. Beyond describing the requirements of the role, what accomplishments might you report? Make sure you have a few notable successes you can point to at the conclusion of your interim assignment.

How will it feel to go back to my previous role?

Several years ago, I had the opportunity to lead a department while the regular leader was on an extended medical leave. I hustled to manage my regular role and hers and, by all accounts, did an admirable job. When she came back, I was miserable. After several months of setting my own agenda, engaging with a broad group of people, and having the freedom to do things the way I wanted, it felt crushing to move from person-in-charge to second-in-command. I was unhappy, she was unhappy, and we never got back into our earlier groove.

An interim role provides an exceptional opportunity to try on and try out for a larger role, and I generally advise colleagues to accept a temporary assignment whenever possible. It can enable you to expand your knowledge, meet new people, and beef up your résumé. Importantly, time spent in an interim appointment can make you feel uncomfortable and even terrified. That can be beneficial because any opportunity to operate in a discomfort zone generally leads to the best learning of all.

However, it is worth noting that interim positions come with serious risks. Because you are not the rightful owner of the real job, you may face unusual scrutiny, especially from those who wanted it for themselves or for someone close to them.

It is an honor to be considered for an interim role, but think strategically before you sign on. Considering the risks and rewards can help you determine whether taking the job or leaving it to someone else is the wiser course.

FIND OUT WHAT THEY ARE SAYING ABOUT YOU

Do you have superior intelligence? Unparalleled technical expertise? Extraordinary vision? If so, you are no doubt wondering: how it is possible to be so talented yet repeatedly unsuccessful when trying to land a bigger job, a higher salary, or a more visible professional association role?

You probably have some theories about that, and I can imagine what they might be. Perhaps you believe your exceptional productivity makes the slackers around you uncomfortable. Peers are just jealous of your laser-like focus. You speak the truth, and most people can't handle hearing it. Decision makers are too dense to recognize your brilliance. Or the always reliable standby: politics are at play.

Those are all reasonable explanations that many of us have posited to make sense of rejection. It is far more comforting to blame others than to explore the possibility that we are the source of our own problems.

Our tendency to blame others is no surprise. We often fail to understand that we're holding ourselves back—because those around us are too afraid or reluctant to tell us what we need to know. They are happy to speak up when our budget figures were added incorrectly, when we have typos on our presentation slides, or when our revenue forecasts seem overly optimistic. But when it comes to commenting on elements of our personal style that make us annoying or even insufferable, everything goes dark. Many of us learn far too late that the personality attributes we consider to be our

strengths have actually become weaknesses, and too many of us really have no idea about how we appear to others.

Consider the following:

- We see ourselves as tenacious. Our colleagues view us as unrelenting.
- We think it is important to be flexible. Our colleagues find us to be unfocused.
- We like to build consensus. Our colleagues claim we are indecisive.
- We believe it is helpful to be direct. Our colleagues consider us caustic.
- We pride ourselves on finding answers. Our colleagues say we expect others to drop everything when we have a problem.
- We know the value of detailed analysis. Our colleagues say we spend too much time on minutiae.

Do any of those sound vaguely familiar? If so, is there anything you can do to identify—and try to temper—what seem like ingrained personality traits?

Some organizations offer 360-degree feedback surveys that provide comments on our styles and approaches from bosses, peers, direct reports, and even clients or customers. If the responses are provided by people who truly care about giving meaningful advice, the results can be quite powerful. So, if you are offered an opportunity to go through this process, give it serious consideration. But you don't have to wait for a formal process to learn how to be more effective. If you are genuinely curious and committed to being more professionally successful, you can use a do-it-yourself approach instead. Here's how:

Step 1. Make a list of at least five people who work with you enough to comment on your personal style. Choose at least two whom you especially admire for their success in navigating their own careers.

Step 2. Tell each person that you are seeking honest feedback and offer to take them to lunch, coffee, or happy hour if they will agree to provide straightforward answers to five questions that you will send in advance. Here are the questions:

- Which of my personal strengths differentiate me most?
- When people compliment me out of earshot, what themes emerge?
- When people criticize me behind my back, what do they say?
- What are two or three things I could start, stop, or change to be more effective?

If you had to choose one thing that might be holding me back professionally, what would it be?

Step 3. During the feedback meeting, listen, take notes, and resist the urge to argue or interrupt. Above all, do not punish your conversation partners for speaking the truth as they see it.

Step 4. Decide how you plan to proceed. Will you reject anything you hear that contradicts the way you see yourself? Or will you try to deal with any issues that your conversation partners were kind and courageous enough to share with you? If you decide to keep going, then move to the next step.

Step 5. Review the themes that emerged and choose one or two of them to work on. Then work them hard. Consider telling a few colleagues what you are trying to change and ask them to call you out (discreetly) when they observe you pontificating in meetings, sending overly pointy messages to the departmental listserv, or engaging in other career-limiting behaviors.

After you have practiced your new behaviors for a while, be sure to get back to your information providers to share your progress and any possible successes that have come your way, thanks to their honest and generous feedback. Then consider a new set of people who will tell you more things that you need to know about yourself. Because there is always more to know.

GET YOUR NAME IN THE CHALICE

Inspiration for navigating career politics can emerge from the most unusual places, among them the city of Rome, where cardinals from around the world convene from time to time to select the next pope. The centuries-old selection process begins once the cardinals are locked inside the Sistine Chapel and ends with a plume of white smoke, the signal that a new pope has been chosen. The selection process is launched when each cardinal writes the name of a colleague on a ballot, trying as much as possible to disguise his handwriting. Each ballot is folded twice and carried to the altar, where it is placed in a large chalice.[1] Votes from the chalice are counted and announced, and the process continues over and over again until one candidate receives two-thirds of the votes. While no rule forbids a cardinal from lobbying for votes or even writing down his own name, the sin of pride makes such actions unseemly.

You might want to remember the cardinals the next time someone asks you to suggest somebody for a job or assignment that you really want. Some of us, conditioned to believe that it is important to express confidence and always ask for what you want, can get burned in a scenario like this. If the question is "Are you interested in this opportunity?" you are free to say you are. But if the question is "Whom might you recommend?" you probably should resist the urge to respond, "Actually, I would like to be considered." The question is often a test, and certain answers can ensure that you fail it.

When faced with an "I'm collecting names" inquiry, your job is not to make a case for the role; rather, it is to get yourself on everyone else's list of possibilities. When your name surfaces repeatedly in the figurative chalice, the decision maker is able to justify selecting you because all of your colleagues agreed that you were the right choice. It works for the pope, and it can work for you.

So how do you get your name in the chalice? It doesn't usually happen without some serious intention, but there is a formula that tends to work for most people.

The first step is to decide what you want and where you might like to do it. Without a sense of direction, it is hard to know how to lay the groundwork for making a career move. The next step is to be visible and have an established track record before the role you want opens up. You want to be positioned as a star before you need that status. Promotions rarely go to people who simply do their current role well. To the degree possible, always do more than expected and be consistently visible. This might mean pursuing especially challenging assignments, seeking a role on a high-profile project team, assuming responsibility for an important project that no one else wants to take on, or engaging in speaking or training sessions that will put you in front of large numbers of people.

As you are busy being consistently impressive, let your well-connected and influential friends and colleagues know about your aspirations. In these conversations, you can ask if they have advice about how to secure the professional or community role you are seeking and then ask them to think of you should they learn of future opportunities. That way, when they are asked by a search firm, professional colleague, or community leader, your name will be at the top of their mind. Should you learn of an opportunity yourself, consider asking a colleague to suggest or nominate you for the role. This is likely to be more successful than pursuing it yourself. When asked to make recommendations, point the askers to those likely to point back right to you: "You know who would really be perfect for this role? [Insert your name here]."

Perhaps the most valuable strategy for getting your name in the chalice is to be helpful and useful to others without an expectation of anything in return. Most of us like to help good people who have been kind or helpful to us in the past. Making an investment in the success of others is often a strategy for elevating our own career prospects. In his book *Give and Take: A Revolutionary Approach to Success*, Wharton School professor Adam Grant recounts several stories of people who supported the careers of others without expecting reciprocity, only to find that their behavior encouraged remarkable generosity in others. Grant shares an especially charming story about a wealthy Australian financier's acts of kindness to someone who did not appear to have the means to repay him that unexpectedly led to more business. "The more I help out, the more successful I become," the financier explained.[2]

While being helpful to others can yield big dividends, you need to do your part to increase your personal visibility, so let trusted colleagues and confidants know that you are ready for a bigger or different role. It is hard for people to help you if they don't know what you want. When you learn about an opportunity, ask two or more colleagues to nominate you for the position. Being recommended for a role is almost always more powerful than expressing interest in it yourself. That said, having several people make nominations will smack of an orchestrated campaign. Be judicious.

When it comes to selecting a pope, active campaigning is considered unseemly, but coalition-building is commonplace. That distinction might be helpful to you. When you are hoping to get your name in the chalice, rely less on lobbying and work instead to position yourself as the people's choice. Make it easy and politically popular to choose you over anyone else.

BEHAVE WELL WHEN YOU'RE NOT THE ONE

The past year has been one of disappointment for three of my favorite people. Each pursued an internal opportunity that seemed like a done deal, only to be notified that the new role was going to someone else. Because all of them were encouraged to apply with some variation of "You'd be perfect for this," they were especially disappointed and surprised when the jobs went to someone else. While they're all dealing with the inevitable sting of rejection, they're struggling more deeply with what feels to them like profound betrayal. It is one thing to be passed over by another organization that does not know you, but when it happens at home, the "sorry, you're not the one" revelation can feel deeply personal.

Given that there are few secrets in most organizations, applying for a new job inside your current workplace is rarely a confidential experience. Colleagues often know when you are a candidate, and they also know when the nod eventually goes to someone else. While my three colleagues were immediately disappointed by not getting the jobs they wanted, they quickly began to ruminate about whether those who knew about their interest in moving up were now ridiculing them for pursuing something big. They felt embarrassed, rejected, and exposed. Two of them began making plans to move because they were convinced that they had lost internal credibility.

I told them they were overreacting and attempted to provide reassuring words. But I am not sure they absorbed what I had to say. I worry that they will use this one experience of rejection to make a quick and uncalculated move to something that is not better. Should they decide to stay, I am concerned that they will use the experience to justify not taking the kinds of future risks we all need to take to move forward. They need to appreciate that the path upward is almost always bumpy; we just don't always see the barriers and setbacks that others face.

If you have been rebuffed for an internal opportunity, consider the following:

There is wide consensus that you should have gotten the job

It is highly possible that everyone, except the final hiring authority, decided that you were the one. One person is not all people, so don't let this decision prompt you to conclude that you have no supporters.

You have captured our attention

Jobs and awards tend to encourage expressions of interest from both the usual and unusual suspects. While "unusual suspects" are not always successful, they are frequently remembered and therefore better positioned for the next opportunity. Don't be afraid to put the universe on notice that you are ready for something bigger.

No one is laughing at you

It is normal to feel exposed after going for a new role in a very public way, but we are not judging you for doing this. It is more likely that you are inspiring us with your courage.

We are waiting to see how you respond

The way you deal with disappointment will be telling, and we are watching for signs of bitterness and defeat. It's okay to express regret, but outrage and profound depression make us nervous. If you can keep it together, everyone will be rooting for you to get the job the next time it comes around.

We want to offer you some advice

Candidates who consider a job rejection as an occasion for learning tend to improve their future prospects, so don't waste the opportunity to request feedback. Let the "chosen one" get settled and then ask those who influenced the hiring decision for guidance on how to position yourself better the next time.[1] You may receive some valuable insights.

Organizations need wise, brave, kind, and ethical people to assume leadership roles, so if you fit that bill, you need to be making your interest in a bigger role known. In the event your expression of interest is rebuffed, consider it an opportunity to demonstrate your tenacity rather than a sign that you were dreaming too big.

PROTECT
YOURSELF

BUILD YOURSELF A FORTRESS

Whenever a leadership transition is in the works, there is a fair amount of chitter-chatter about who will stay and who will go. Will the incoming leader fire all the incumbents and bring in a new team to ensure the loyalty of all lieutenants, or will there be an effort to retain those who can support a smooth transition from the past to the future? After witnessing a good number of leadership transitions in various sectors, I have discovered some secrets of those who seem to have Herculean staying power. I call them the protected people.

While possessing a seemingly-impossible-to-replace form of expertise can guard against banishment, most protected people enjoy a sense of safety because they have built a personal fortress that makes them safe from advancement or attack. A fortress, of course, is heavily protected and impenetrable. Slings, arrows, boulders, cannonballs, rotten cabbages—nothing gets through a fortress if the walls are thick enough, tall enough, and strong enough. So how do these individuals build a fortress, and what lessons can we learn from them to create political and professional protection for ourselves?

Here are five ways protected people build their fortresses:

Strategy 1: They establish a reputation for supporting the success of others

On a regular basis, this might mean making introductions, offering writing advice, sharing strategic guidance, providing early alerts, or removing barriers. When engaging with a new leader, protected people are often those who can reveal which group has real power, which community members require an immediate return call and who can wait awhile, how to sell an idea, and the names of those who can be trusted and those who cannot.

Supporting others offers protection in several ways. First, it creates a sense of reciprocity: they helped me, so I should repay the favor. Second, all leaders want to be successful, so it behooves them to surround themselves with those who can support that success. Third, when a person is valued or even cherished for being an honest and reliable go-to resource, the new leader will appear vindictive and capricious for casting them out.

Strategy 2: They have a network that is broad and deep

There are few things more professionally dangerous than being isolated and alone. Without supporters, we are easy targets. Arbitrary acts of persecution can be carried out safely when there is no support team to offer pushback or assign penalties. The protected people intentionally and energetically forge mutually beneficial relationships with a diverse network that includes key influencers who will speak out should harm appear imminent.

Strategy 3: They pay attention

The ability to connect dots and makes sense of our environment is a rare and valuable skill. The protected people know who is actually or metaphorically sleeping with whom, who is still angry about a dispute that occurred a decade ago, and the pet peeves and pet causes of those with power and influence—and they use this valuable currency to trade with others.

Strategy 4: They are not obviously evil

It is one thing to be voraciously ambitious and shrewdly calculating, but those who are obvious in their mistreatment of others don't usually last all that long. Protected people know that treating others badly is frowned upon, so when they want to inflict harm or simply have an unpopular decision to implement, they make sure someone else's fingerprints are on their dirty deeds.

Strategy 5: They make sure everyone knows they have ammunition

Some protected people make it clear that they have powerful and potentially embarrassing information. They know which colleague was convicted of stealing money from her sorority while in college, which department director had an affair with the corporate attorney's spouse, and the exact month a certain purchasing officer leaked information that helped his brother-in-law secure the digital advertising contract. Rather than reporting bad behavior, the protected people offer to keep things quiet and occasionally mention how terrible it would be for the news to get out.

Some of these survival techniques seem strategic, while others are clearly unscrupulous. Must you be Machiavellian to ensure survival during a leadership transition or manage your long-term career success? Is it truly a good practice to dig up dirt, assign our hard decisions to those lower down the organizational food chain, or threaten others with exposure? You know that it is not and that it is possible to be professionally successful without engaging in political warfare. Being honest and honorable may not always offer obvious short-term dividends, but it tends to be a wise long-term career strategy that leads to being surrounded by supportive allies rather than cowering sycophants.

As for those who make a habit of using dirty tricks, they usually run out of luck when their survival approach becomes obvious to enough people. This often prompts a question: do you have an obligation to help others see who is truly deceitful, dishonest, and even maniacal? Perhaps, but there are serious risks involved. Before embarking on this kind of crusade, you need to gather an army, a suit of armor, and some mighty sharp tools. It is not easy to chip away at the bricks of a fortress that is protecting someone evil inside.

DON'T LET MEAN PEOPLE DESTROY YOUR CAREER

A few years ago, a professional organization offered me an opportunity that was hard to resist: the chance to speak to emerging leaders on the topic of my choice. I proposed the title "Don't Let Mean People Destroy Your Career" and set to work crafting the pithy, inspiring talk they wanted. I was excited about the topic because I have been both a target and an unwitting protector of mean people in recent years, and I thought this would be an opportunity to think through some of the mistakes I have made in dealing with them.

I began my talk by listing some of the attributes of mean people. I noted how they tend to steal credit, spread rumors, cut in line, hog resources, and intentionally give out misinformation. I described their propensity to criticize with vigor and abandon to demonstrate their superiority and everyone else's unworthiness. I acknowledged that my list was incomplete but would suffice for the purposes of our discussion. My plan was not to focus on what it is like to be a target of mean acts but to instead describe our responsibilities as leaders when we discover that we have a mean person reporting to us.

When most of us assumed leadership roles, I told my audience, we imagined ourselves to be compassionate people with values and standards. It would not occur to us to intentionally hire or forge partnerships with mean people, and if we discovered that we had done so accidentally, we

would certainly try to make things right. As I uttered these words, everyone in the audience nodded in agreement.

And then I revealed my main point: while most of us do not intentionally hire mean people, we tend to keep them once we discover their meanness, even though their personal values are not aligned with our own.

While giving this talk, I admitted that I had three primary reasons for keeping a handful of mean people around for too long. First, the mean people weren't mean to me. In fact, when we were together, these people were intellectually stimulating, generous with ideas and assistance, and often remarkably thoughtful. For a while, I actually thought other people were just jealous of the mean people's particular talents and were only complaining to maximize their own status. But eventually, the meanness became obvious to me, and I had to acknowledge the second reason I was not taking action: each of the mean people had technical expertise that would be difficult and prohibitively expensive to replace.

Believing it would be easier to fix the offenders than to find new people, I pushed to understand what drove the mean people to behave badly. I reasoned that if I could make sense of those motivations, I could design an intervention to turn the behavior around. Through a series of painful conversations—in which I expressed support but explained that their jobs were on the line if they didn't turn things around—I learned that each of the mean people had been shaped by unhappy life experiences that had made them feel small, insignificant, or unloved. That changed my worldview, and I began to consider them wounded people who deserved to be saved from self-destruction. This brought me to my third reason for failing to take action: my discomfort with casting out people who were so clearly misbehaving in response to psychic wounds. *I will not abandon them,* I told myself. *I will save them!*

Feeling ambitious and heroic, I embarked upon a campaign to highlight and eliminate the offending behaviors. I asked the mean people to pay close attention to how others responded to them, encouraged them to seek honest feedback from colleagues, and met with them regularly to strategize and discuss their progress. I was convinced that if we held a mirror to the behavior and encouraged a bit of reflection, the mean people would see the error of their ways and be transformed.

I am such a dreamer

As you might have guessed, none of the campaigns was successful. One of the mean people explained how difficult it was to work with intellectual inferiors. Another talked repeatedly of the importance of maintaining high standards. Yet another argued emphatically that if colleagues felt intimidated or uncomfortable, it was their problem, not hers. One day, feeling particularly despondent and out of options, I called a leadership development consultant for advice on what these mean people needed. "One word," he said. "Therapy."

He might have been right, but that was not my call to make. Furthermore, I am not sure therapy would have even been all that beneficial. Bad things have happened to a lot of us, and we are not all miserable people. I have come to believe that mean people don't have to be mean; they choose to be mean. And choices have consequences. My mean people chose not to change, and I eventually chose to let them try to find new jobs.

Unfortunately, I took too long to send them on their way, and that was the point I wanted to make in wrapping up my talk. I cautioned about the dangers of failing to be strong and decisive when it comes to dealing with mean people and warned that being compassionate for too long can eventually undermine our professional credibility. Severing relationships with mean people swiftly, and without offering them a chance at reformation, is unfair to them. But taking action too slowly is unfair to everyone else. And, in some cases, inaction can send the message that everyone else also has a permission slip to behave badly.

A few weeks after my talk, I had an unpleasant email exchange with a member of my team that gave me an opportunity to demonstrate my new resolve to act quickly and decisively in response to bad behavior. While the old me might have stood back, hoping the acerbic author would eventually repent for the nasty-gram, the new me jumped out of my chair to pay a visit to the writer. I imagined an uncomfortable yet productive dialogue that would end in an expression of remorse and a promise to be more civil in the future.

What I got was something quite different: "Seriously? You've finally found religion and are going to hold me accountable? I figure I'm owed about five years of bad behavior given what you allowed [Another Mean Person] to get away with for so long." A little dramatic? I think so. Insubordination? I'll let you decide. But the conversation was certainly proof that my inaction regarding one person emboldened another.

As I have reflected on who might be worth saving and on my own missteps in trying to chart the right path when faced with challenging people, I have concluded that it is best to invest resources in those who are curious about how they are perceived and not in those who want to prove that what everyone else is saying about them is incorrect.

Here's a quick test: when you express concern about someone's bad behavior on the job, is that employee's response characterized by regret and curiosity ("I can't believe I have had this effect; is there a way I can turn this around?") or by anger and defensiveness ("Who has complained about me? What were their exact words?").

If it's the former, do your best to offer assistance. If it's the latter, start planning for the employee's exit.

If a colleague's difficult personality is giving you trouble, my little test may be insufficient to move you to action. In the back of your mind, you may be questioning whether your instincts are on target. Trust me, they probably are. Perhaps it will be helpful to understand why you are hesitating to act. If you are like most people, it is likely that you are thinking about one or more of the following:

It is hard to measure mean

We can count dollars raised, patients seen, and meals served, but it's hard to quantify bad behavior. How many snippy emails are too many? How much sarcasm is excessive? When do high expectations become abusive demands?

I have invested a lot in this person

Sunk costs are those expenses (time, money, psychic energy) that we have invested in the past and cannot recover.[1] We often treat mean people like problematic used cars: "I just bought a new transmission and won't recover what I spent if I sell it now." With people, the costs can include relocation expenses, start-up costs, and time spent training, orienting, creating ideas, and making introductions.

I hired this person for a reason

Something led us to decide that our problem person was "the one" when we made the offer of employment: an impressive portfolio, special expertise, a track record of good ideas, an innovative way of seeing the world. Saying goodbye often represents dashed dreams for the future and immediate worries about who will do the work that needs to be done.

I don't see the bad behavior

Most mean people are clever enough to know how to behave at least some of the time, and they reserve their very best behavior for the people to whom they report. "But they aren't like that with me" is something I have heard from others and something that I have said myself.

I know that the meanness is related to hurt, insecurity, or trauma[2,3]

A quick Google search on "mean people" will lead you to a multitude of discussions about the need to treat them with compassion because they are in pain and trying to build themselves up by making others feel small. You can certainly show compassion to the person who is hurting, but what will become of everyone else who is being made to suffer?

When it comes to dealing with mean people, quick, decisive action is important. Name the behavior that is causing problems. Establish expectations. Be clear about consequences. Set timelines for improvement, and don't be fooled by temporary niceness. While many people are incapable of transforming their personalities, it is worth giving everyone a chance. Every once in a while, we can be happily surprised.

RECOGNIZE WHEN YOU ARE THE WEAKEST LINK

While sitting in a committee that was only tangentially related to the kind of work I did every day, I asked myself, *What am I doing here?* I had nothing helpful to ask or add, and the conversation was highly technical. I felt out of place and strangely incompetent. As others around the table talked with great passion and animation, I pondered how I could gracefully get myself off this committee's roster. *This is boring and painful,* I said to myself.

A week later, that sense of profound incompetence returned as I accompanied my daughter for an escape room experience in Nashville, Tennessee. I began the adventure with a fair sense of confidence and optimism. I imagined using my reasoning and negotiation skills to break my team free from a pretend prison in fewer than the sixty minutes we were allotted. I would save the day—because I do so love saving the day. As our group was combined with another family, it became obvious that only a few of us actually were old enough to have high-school diplomas. I felt a weighty sense of obligation. *Looks like I will have to do the heavy lifting,* I thought to myself as we were escorted into our cells.

As the prison bars clanked to a close, I sprang into action. My first contribution was immediate, and I proudly displayed a clue I found by applying my superior investigation skills. Then I tied a complicated knot that was required

to complete the next assignment. Mission accomplished; I was on fire!

And then, for the next fifty-six minutes, I offered nothing of value. Every suggestion was a dead end that simply set the team back. Apparently, my mind is not made for cracking codes, solving puzzles, or finding hints inside journals with bad handwriting. It quickly became clear that I would be most helpful if I shut up and started taking orders from people who were several decades younger than me. So I did.

We ended our hour together one clue shy of victory, but we were assured, "This is definitely the hardest challenge here." People in Nashville are very nice.

Feeling defeated after the experience, I reflected on a book I read on the plane ride to Nashville: *Simple Sabotage: A Modern Field Manual for Detecting & Rooting Out Everyday Behaviors That Undermine Your Workplace.*[1] Authors Robert M. Galford, Bob Frisch, and Cary Greene assert that committees and project teams are most effective when they are populated with people who can serve in one of four roles that start with W:

Worker. Someone who is there to get things done

Wisdom. A person who has smart ideas or perspectives to share

Wealth. A person with resources to contribute

Window Dressing. Someone whose participation increases the group's status

As I read this book, I reflected on the technical committee where I felt oddly out of place. It was suddenly obvious that I was merely window dressing. That group wanted the value of my name and position, not any actual ideas or perspectives from me. Then I considered my escape room adventure and determined that I was playing the role of a fifth and undesirable W: the *weakest link*.

Noting my sense of despondency, my highly logical and clue-savvy daughter encouraged me to focus on what I did right during our pretend-prison experience. So as a public service to those of you who may one day find that you are the weakest link in a team or group, I offer you the following advice:

Give ideas, but don't insist they be pursued

My daughter noted that my ideas were consistently flawed, but they did provide the group with a number of possibilities to reject. "We knew that if you suggested something, we should almost do the opposite," she explained, trying to make me feel like I had contributed something of value.

Stay out of the way

During the course of our lives, we will be inserted into situations for which we are unprepared, unqualified, or inferior. Rather than trying to demonstrate our value, it sometimes makes sense to keep quiet and let others take charge of the situation.

Recognize the people who figure things out

Breaking out of fake prison, like leading a complex project team or a politically charged committee, can be emotionally challenging. Expressing appreciation to those doing the heavy lifting gives them the energy to keep going.

Whenever possible, attempt to extricate yourself

It is psychologically taxing to be the loser member of a group. Offer a gracious apology and move on. Most everyone will be happy and relieved.

Our contributions to any endeavor will always be variable, but when we know our participation is slowing things down or mucking things up, we can earn points by moving on. It is always better to be the one who leaves voluntarily than the one whom everyone has to work around.

CONSIDER THE RISKS OF ACTING RESPONSIBLY

Spreading gossip about your boss's bad habits, using the departmental printer to produce political campaign brochures for your best friend, forging expense receipts—these are reckless activities that can get you in trouble and damage your career, and you are certainly smart enough to avoid them. Why? Because you are highly responsible.

You know that being highly responsible means acting with integrity. It means being conscientious and judicious with resources. It means offering appropriate warnings, keeping others safe from harm, and choosing the right course of action even when it may make you unpopular. If you consider yourself to be more responsible than others, it may come as a surprise that in many organizations, acting with integrity can derail rather than enhance your career.

Here are five examples of behaviors that seem highly responsible but may actually harm your career.

Alerting people to what failed before

Your new division head wants to redesign the training approach for new hires and has mapped out a plan to launch the redesign quickly. You agree that the approach needs a makeover but note the division head's new plan looks remarkably similar to the failed effort that was attempted six years ago. You feel obligated to detail the many reasons the earlier redesign was unsuccessful and provide details

about how it contributed to the former division head's ignominious departure.

What to consider instead. People who think they have developed novel ideas typically resent those who utter the phrase, "That will never work" or "We tried that before," so banish those words from your vocabulary. Before pointing out all the reasons this plan will fail, think about whether the world has changed since the last proposal was introduced and the chances that it might be better received today. If you truly see danger ahead, position yourself as a resource rather than a naysayer and offer the division head a list of lessons learned from the last redesign that might be helpful in moving this new effort forward.

Standing on principle

It is good to have values and opinions about what is right and wrong, and every organization needs people courageous enough to speak truth to power. There is no question that those brave enough to question the integrity of a course of action can prompt a group to make better decisions. But constant position taking can be perceived as disruptive and may earn you a label as a person who is inflexible and unreasonable.

What to consider instead. First, recognize that some issues don't matter enough to waste valuable political capital. Even when an issue is truly important, it is best to use outrage sparingly. In general, most groups respond better to inquiry than advocacy, so use this approach instead. Rather than enumerating the many reasons an idea is flawed, ask a series of well-spaced questions to help others realize they are headed down a dangerous path. If that doesn't work, express your concern about the direction of the conversation as a strategy for going on record about your position and then spend the rest of the time listening. It is possible you will learn something that changes your mind.

Honoring all requests

Do you find everything interesting? Do you think you are smarter than most people and therefore especially qualified to add value to every group you join? Is it possible that declining requests is uncomfortable for you? There may be many motivations that drive you to join every committee, accept every request, and agree to every speaking or meeting invitation, but being spread too thin will compromise your ability to focus on your most strategic work. Saying yes to everything may also deny colleagues and those who report to you an opportunity to learn, grow, and increase their own visibility. It is also worth noting that hypervisibility may also create envy among those who are less likely to be invited or included.

What to consider instead. Ask yourself:

"Is my participation essential, or could someone else do this instead?"

"What is my motivation for accepting this request?"

"Who might benefit from taking my place?"

Focusing on getting things done rather than fostering relationships

Progress is important to you, and you believe honoring deadlines to be essential. So rather than go to lunch with your colleagues or join an occasional happy hour gathering, you work and work and work. You think you are being responsible. Your colleagues likely find you annoying and standoffish.[1]

It is good to have a reputation for being reliable and delivering good work, but being known as the person who works more and harder than anyone else has a way of creating a distance between you and others. The people who work with you may feel pressure to mirror your behavior and come to resent you for it. More importantly, working all the time may compromise your ability to build relationships with people who can actually help you get more done.

What to consider instead. Forging trust-based relationships with a diverse network may actually make you more productive by giving you new insights or someone to call upon when you need a favor. Certainly, having a psychological support team is critical for most of us. If relationship nurturing does not come naturally to you, make connecting with others a part of your weekly task list. You may want to set a goal of one lunch with others, one walking meeting, and three quick workplace chats or email check-ins each week. The visibility will be good for you, and a bit of interaction may help you learn something that will increase your impact. Remember also that staying connected with those outside your organization is as important as cultivating relationships inside it.

Insisting on integrity

You have high standards, and you expect your leaders to be role models. When they disappoint you, you may feel it necessary to point out their failings to others. But here's the thing: that feedback usually makes it back to the leader you are criticizing. When that happens, you may be shunned, be eliminated, or at least become the target of a counterattack.

What to consider instead. Be a person of integrity yourself and appear puzzled or surprised by ethical lapses by others. Rather than condemning behavior, express curiosity about it and let others reach their own conclusions. Resist the urge to utter disparaging remarks.

Do these career sabotage examples look familiar to you? Have you noticed these behaviors in yourself or others? Being highly responsible is a valuable trait, but the way we express our personal values can often work against us, especially in highly political environments that prize "going along to get along." If you find yourself losing ground in your current environment and want to remain a part of it, begin to observe the behaviors of those who seem to be doing better than you are. Who are their allies? What is their ratio of heads-down work to socializing with others? How do they handle conflicting opinions? When do they take stands, and when do they let issues slide? The organizational navigation tools they are using may also work for you.

LINK THEIR SUCCESS TO YOUR SURVIVAL

Envy is a dangerous emotion, and there is a growing body of research that suggests coworker envy can compromise the success and career prospects of high performers.[1] Strong performers raise the bar for others in the workgroup, and lower performers often find themselves not wanting to exert additional effort or incapable of demonstrating the intellectual capacity to keep up with the workgroup achiever. To protect their jobs or their status, envious coworkers may engage in a series of moves to undermine the credibility of the high performer, intentionally sabotage their work products, or attempt to drive them out of the organization altogether.[2]

If you are a high performer, how can you meet your own high standards without alienating colleagues? Consider linking their success to yours.

Begin by ensuring that you have talents, abilities, connections, and information that others need but do not possess. Then offer them to coworkers to support them in looking good. I saw this in action with a woman I will call Tamara, who had exceptional technical expertise but struggled to write compelling proposals or create excitement when she presented her ideas. Despite her challenges, she had a strong network and a fair amount of influence. She often criticized her newest colleague, Esteban, for having what she called "voodoo mind powers" because his less technically sophisticated ideas and proposals were consistently applauded and adopted by senior leaders.

Recognizing Tamara's frustration and sensing that he was her emerging target, Esteban offered to edit her writing and proposals. "I have a few tricks in phrasing and idea organization that seem to work," he explained. "I'd be happy to review your first drafts if that would be helpful." She agreed.

Esteban noted that Tamara seemed to repeat the same writing and composing errors, and she loaded her presentations with far too much data. He debated whether to teach her how to address these tendencies or simply improve her work. For several months, he rewrote her memos, proposals, and presentations, hoping to create a sense of dependency. "It was a lot more work for me," he noted, "but I needed to move her perception of me as someone who was a threat to someone who was vital to her success." His plan worked better than he had imagined. Not only did Esteban make Tamara an ally, but it bolstered her visibility and self-confidence and gave her the courage to seek and secure a role at a new organization. Esteban neutralized a threat and was eventually able to welcome a new, more secure colleague.

A woman I will call Herminia tried something similar when it became obvious that just doing her job—reporting on organizational metrics—was making a senior executive with an underperforming unit look bad. Rather than accept accountability for the performance numbers, the senior executive began to undermine Herminia's credibility, questioning her data sources, analytical abilities, and personal motivations. Given the senior executive's status, longevity, and connections, Herminia knew that her job was the one at risk, even though she was just revealing the truth. Instead of sticking to her position, Herminia worked to build a relationship with the senior executive. Together, they worked through the reporting methodology, and Herminia was able to provide the senior executive with some ideas about how to share results about his other higher-performing units while creating a roadmap for turning around the numbers in the unit that was struggling. Eventually, the senior executive became known as the most data-oriented member of the organization's leadership team and was regularly applauded for the way he was able to present data in visually compelling ways—all thanks to Herminia's behind-the-scenes work, of course. Herminia eventually groomed a successor and left the organization. And her strongest reference? The senior executive who had originally tormented her.

You do not need a nemesis to employ the tactic of creating interdependency. Being generally helpful to all of your colleagues will elevate their success and help you build a network of fans and supporters who will speak well of you, watch your back, and offer you help in the event you need it.[3]

Needing to do more than one's fair share of work without receiving extra credit is frustrating, but it can be an essential career survival strategy, especially in highly political environments in which slackers and underperformers may use their positions, influence, and networks for personal protection. Your goal is to stay safe until you can get out, and being especially useful is often the best strategy.

DON'T BE CAPTIVATED BY CHARISMA

When it comes to making a hiring decision or offering a recommendation on a candidate you have interviewed, do you consider yourself objective? Do you focus on the candidate's qualifications, or do you fall into bias traps that lead you to choose people much like you? Have you found yourself expressing a preference for candidates who seem light on substance but heavy on style? If you are like most people, you lean toward big personalities that exude high levels of confidence.[1]

You may tell yourself that people who express confidence do so because they are highly qualified, but you will be deluding yourself because there is no proven correlation between expressing confidence and actually possessing competence,[2] although we tell ourselves a different story. It is common to confuse confidence with competence and to consider charismatic individuals as uniquely qualified to lead our organizations or tackle difficult challenges. Too often, we gravitate toward those who are charming, dynamic, and engaging, even when they lack the skills or intellect to effectively lead us into the future.

I must admit that I am a member of the Charisma Club because I have a well-known preference for sparkly people. I love confident speakers, bold thinkers, and gregarious conversationalists. While overly theatrical personalities and excessive bravado annoy me, I am drawn to candidates with a sense of pizazz. Self-confidence appeals to me, and I lean

129

toward convivial speakers who have the confidence to work a room and express provocative views. I also like a good sense of humor, excellent posture, eye contact, and a sense of magnetism. But over the course of my career, I have come to understand that many of the characteristics that make candidates appealing to me are often the same attributes that lead me to eventually be disappointed in them. Because it is easy for me to gloss over the absence of substance when entranced by style, I have too often pushed for the candidate who dazzled me rather than the one who was actually qualified to get the job done. More than a few times, I have had to clean up after a "star" I championed failed to deliver. I don't want you to make the same mistake.

For a long time, I thought I had a personality defect that led me to fall in love with big talkers and low deliverers, but then I read Thomas Chamorro-Premuzic's book *Why Do So Many Incompetent Men Becine Leaders? (And How to Fix It).* His book is less about incompetent men and more about how we tend to be dangerously mesmerized by people with charisma. Chamorro-Premuzic explains that we are often drawn to those who demonstrate high levels of self-assurance, and we gravitate toward those who make bold declarations and discuss big plans. It is only after we have worked with these people for a while that the magic spell wears off, and we discover that confident big talkers are not always capable of delivering anything of consequence. Chamorro-Premuzic notes, "There is a world of difference between the personality traits and behaviors it takes to be *chosen* as a leader and the traits and skills you need to be *able* to lead effectively."[3]

This is not to say that we should reject people who are charismatic, because charisma is a highly valuable attribute, especially in certain highly visible roles and often in times of crisis. But charisma is not required for every role, and it is certainly not the most important attribute for any position. Given this, why do we allow ourselves to be so entranced by people with energy and charm? There is evidence that evolutionary signaling may be at play.

In their *Leadership Quarterly* article "Charisma as Signal: An Evolutionary Perspective on Charismatic Leadership," Allen Grabo, Brian R. Spisak, and Markvan Vugt assert that "the function of charismatic leadership is to enable followers to swiftly coordinate their actions by rallying behind the leader, thus allowing them to overcome a pressing challenge that would otherwise be insoluble."[4] While this might have been important hundreds of years ago when there were deer to be killed and a charismatic leader could mobilize everyone to participate in the hunt, today we have grocery stores. More importantly, our complex problems cannot be solved by blindly following a single individual. We need multiple perspectives and inputs to address our most intractable challenges today. So, much as our desire to consume as many calories as possible when we find a food source is no longer in our best interest, perhaps our proclivity to select charismatic leaders is another evolutionary drive that no longer serves us.

Leadership and organizational behavior researcher Margarita Mayo has found that we turn toward charismatic leaders in times of duress.[5] When things are difficult, we want to be "rescued" and offered easy fixes. This is when we are most likely to seek out those who make lofty promises, appear to have superhuman abilities, or possess the capacity to make us feel better about our current situation. So the next time you are in the process of selecting a new member of your organization, consider whether the current state of affairs is perilous or disconcerting and thereby prompting you to choose someone who seems to have savior powers.

When we are in crisis or facing a very uncertain future, it is normal to hunger for star power when we would actually be better served by humility and a sense of open-mindedness. Organizational research repeatedly demonstrates that humble leaders produce better results than huge personalities because they encourage collaboration and express appreciation for the contributions of others.[6] More humble leaders are also more likely to share honest information in times of distress. Berkeley University economist Benjamin E. Hemalin asserts that charismatic leaders are often tempted to substitute charm for action and to hide bad news to keep followers positively fired up.[7] But here's the challenge: when we are navigating complexity, we need more honest conversation, not less.

Given that we are naturally drawn to people who may not be good for us, how do we break our tendency to lean toward charismatic leaders who may be ill equipped to deliver what we need?

We can begin by being open to the personality characteristics that appeal to us and how they may bias our assessment of a candidate's intelligence, analytical abilities, and strength in leveraging the assets of others. We also need to be more rigorous as we assess candidate credentials and qualifications. We need to know what they have done in the past, not what they claim they would do in the future. Importantly, we need to learn more about how they approach complex challenges and whether they have the stamina to endure hardship and the intellectual bandwidth to engage in complex problem solving. We should also explore whether they have a track record of sharing credit and whether they are sufficiently secure and humble to consider the perspectives of others. We do not accomplish this with breezy conversations with softball questions like "Tell us about your vision of our industry for the next five years" or "What do you hope to achieve within your first one hundred and eighty days?" These inquiries rarely provide evidence of true leadership capacity.

Imagine, instead, asking candidates how they have worked through especially challenging situations in the past or might handle a looming organizational crisis. What would you want to hear from someone answering this question? A tested, competent, community-building leader will generally describe plans to bring together thinking partners with varied perspectives, ask questions, assess the situation, consider multiple scenarios, and test various strategies. An overly confident and charismatic leader will too often rely on instincts to guide the path forward and stress the value of unified action. This might be the right approach for tracking down a four-legged animal but is less effective in creatively addressing various forms of industry disruption.

Because I know that I am drawn to captivating personalities, I make it a regular practice to admit this whenever I am asked to hire or weigh in on a candidate. Many of my colleagues have heard me say, "I tend to fall in love with sparkly people, so I need you to check me on whether this person is smart or simply hypnotizing me." I'm not proud that I have to say this, but it generally starts an important conversation and allows us to probe deeply when we hear each other say things like, "She won me over immediately" or "I felt comfortable with him the minute he walked in the room." It is comments like these that often suggest that we are being played and that our unconscious bias is encouraging us to choose style over substance.

CONSIDER WHY THEY AREN'T CALLING OUT BAD BEHAVIOR

Frustrating colleagues come in many forms and demonstrate many different behaviors. Sometimes they hijack a meeting by constantly interrupting. They might intentionally humiliate or bully others. Perhaps they are overly aggressive in fighting for what they want or in trying to motivate others. Maybe it's something more subtle: they simply avoid their share of the work and expect others to do it for them.

It is one thing to recognize this bad behavior but something quite different to confront it. Many colleagues and organizational leaders struggle to address problematic behavior even when they recognize the effect it is having on others. Why is that?

One factor that makes many people reluctant to speak up is self-doubt. They may ask themselves, *Am I being overly sensitive?* or *Am I imagining things?* As a target of the bad behavior or even a witness to it, look for opportunities to express curiosity or confusion about the bad behavior to make it clear that it is a definite pattern that cannot be ignored.

Status or power differentials may make it awkward or difficult to confront troubling behavior. Perhaps the person who is misbehaving has more seniority or influential connections. In certain settings, those with "superstar" status tend to get away with behavior that would not be tolerated by others. It can be hard to confront someone who has more power or status, so if you are an advisor to the person who is reluctant to take action, consider suggesting they ask a higher-status colleague to step in.

It is quite common to let bad behavior go unchecked because of the fear of losing hard-to-replace expertise. It can seem safer and easier to remain quiet than to lose the one person who knows how to navigate the contracting process, extract data from the enterprise information system, or use contacts to score reservations at otherwise inaccessible restaurants. The lesson for all of us is to make sure there is more than one person who knows how to do anything that needs to be done.

Fear of sabotage can also make it scary to call out bad behavior. Over the years, I have talked to a lot of managers who have problematic employees, and I often give what I consider to be pretty good advice about how to start an honest conversation. As I am walking these folks through a script, they often put their hand out as a sign for me to stop talking. "I can't do that," they tell me. Then they go on to explain their fear that they will pay dearly for engaging in honest conversation. One supervisor once said, "I could see her coming into the lab in the middle of the night and killing all my cell lines." Another said, "He has the power to wipe all the files from our shared drive." Yet another let me know, "She goes to temple with the chair of our board. I can't risk making her angry."

Sheer exhaustion can dampen the energy required to address bad behavior. There are times when repeated slights or other forms of bad behavior seem too frequent to call out over and over again. Likely arguments about the truth and inaccurate perceptions may feel like too much work, so bad behavior continues because it just feels easier to let it go.

It is easy to judge a colleague or leader who fails to address troubling behavior, but it may be helpful to consider why they are failing to engage. Understanding the dynamics at play may position you to offer the support and strategies they need to take action. Being an ally rather than an evaluator can position you as a trusted advisor, and that is a valuable status to have.

BE BETTER THAN YOUR BACKSTABBERS

While working on a project, a colleague I like and trust sent me a text from a meeting she was in: "Guess who is throwing you under the bus right now?"

"No!" I texted back. "Who? What now?"

Thanks to some fast finger work, I provided the real facts about the current meeting topic, and my texting partner was able to relay them to defend my honor. The crisis was averted, and the benefits of cultivating a guardian-angel network were once again revealed. But cultivating such a network is hard work. And ensuring that every gathering is populated by at least one person who will have your back is an impossible task. So what are the best ways to manage those people who seem intent on tearing you down?

Before we can manage backstabbers, we must seek first to understand them. In my experience, backstabbers usually extend their claws for one of the following reasons:

- They are highly ambitious but politically unsophisticated. They think making others look small is the fastest path to looking big.
- They want to eliminate competition and believe that publicly challenging their target's integrity or expertise is a way to make that person vulnerable professionally.
- Their professional qualifications and ability to deliver are in question, so they feel a need to deflect

demands for accountability by calling into question the track records of others.

- They are highly insecure and want to diminish the status of those who appear to be more professionally successful.
- They feel threatened when their competence is questioned.

Most of the backstabbers I know are insecure and maladjusted people who do not believe they can survive on their own merits; that is why they spend so much time trying to eliminate their perceived competition. Knowing that our backstabbers are often haunted by anxiety and insecurity, should we forgive them based on our understanding that their behavior is driven by an inner turmoil they wrestle to control each day? I don't think so. While we can express compassion for the demons that haunt our back-stabbers, malicious actions should lead to negative consequences, at least according to my view of the world.

In her *Harvard Business Review* article "How to Handle a Colleague Who's a Jerk When the Boss Isn't Around," Amy Jen Su offers some sound advice. Don't take bad behavior personally, she advises, because you are probably not the jerk's only target: "When you see the behavior, take a step back and be a spectator to what's going on. It's easy to assume we're onstage as a victim in this person's game; in truth, it's much more about your colleague's lack of self-awareness, insecurity, or past experiences."[1]

While you are on your metaphorical balcony observing the situation, consider whether it makes sense to call out the bad behavior or involve others in the dispute. Su notes that if the behavior is just annoying but has no real impact, it's probably worth letting go. But what if the backstabber's actions or comments pose a true threat to your career or reputation?

Often, expressing curiosity rather than demonstrating outrage is the best strategy. Say something like this to the backstabber: "I understand you've told several people that I am not pulling my weight on our project. I wish you had shared that with me directly, but let's talk about it now. Help me understand your specific concerns."

Or, to your boss: "My partner on the communication strategy project has told several people that I haven't been honoring my commitments. Because I assembled the committee, led the information-gathering process, and wrote the final report, I don't think that assessment is fair, and I'm confused about why she would say this. I just wanted to let you know that I will be talking to her directly soon. Do you have any advice for me when I have that conversation?"

You might also consider trying to win the backstabber over. In their research, Nathanael Fast and Serena Chen found that offering words of affirmation to a backstabber has the power to diminish their aggressiveness. Offering praise or expressing gratitude for something your backstabber has done can increase their self-confidence and reduce their likelihood of lashing out at you. This might not feel like a sincere move, but it might increase your personal safety.

Regardless of whether you confront the backstabber or attempt to make this person an ally, follow Su's advice and resist the urge to strike back. Instead, try to learn from the experience, because backstabbers can teach us a lot. By observing their behavior closely, we can learn framing, storytelling, inquiry skills, and self-promotion tactics. By watching backstabbers in action, we can also learn what matters most to them, uncover whom they consider to be both allies and members of the enemy camp, and how they handle those who make demands for evidence when accusations are uttered.

So instead of getting angry about our backstabbers, let's consider them research subjects. A little objective distance creates a feeling of control, and when we're wearing an emotional shield of armor, it is harder for backstabbers to pierce us with their pointy daggers.

GETTING THINGS DONE

LEAD FROM WHERE YOU ARE

One day, I was in a meeting where there was complaining. I mean a lot of complaining. According to the people in the conversation, their leadership was clueless, most of the employees were incompetent, and the few people with real intelligence were too beaten down to drive meaningful change. According to those doing the bulk of the talking, the organization was sinking fast, and there was nothing to be done about it. It was pathetic and depressing, and it led me to wonder what made this crowd so dispirited and seemingly helpless. After a bit of pondering, I decided there were two dynamics at play.

The first was that the complainers truly had no idea about the levers of organizational change. They assumed that if a manager uttered the phrase "That's impossible," she was speaking the truth.

Those of us who understand organizational politics know "That's impossible" and "That's prohibited by policy" are generally code phrases for "What you're asking for feels like too much work, so let me convince you that it can't be done."

A proper response to such stonewalling is not "Oh, okay. Well, I thought I'd ask." The proper response is, "Why?" Over and over again.[1]

The second dynamic at work was that the group of complainers didn't appreciate the personal power they possessed both individually and collectively to make change possible. They assumed they had to be anointed as leaders or given

143

special authority before they could start behaving like people with the power to make things happen. Faulty assumption.

I am always surprised by those who would prefer to settle for discomfort rather than challenge the status quo, especially when challenging the status quo is a relatively risk-free option. The path to a better future usually seems quite straightforward to me: Identify an issue. Confirm that I am not the only one who thinks there is a problem. Identify options. Figure out who has the power to fix things if I can't do it myself. Convince those with fixing power that making things better is in their own self-interest. *Voilà*—five steps to a solution!

In an interview about encouraging organizational change, Harry M. Kraemer, a clinical professor of strategy at Northwestern University's Kellogg School of Management, urged people to stop waiting to be given permission to act and offered five suggestions:
- Lead from where you are.
- Start offering solutions.
- Do your research.
- Build your network.
- Encourage future leaders.[2]
- Kramer offers sound advice. Let's consider each of his recommendations.

Lead from where you are

Kraemer is right. You don't need to have formal authority or followers to take a stand. Stop waiting. Get moving.

Start offering solutions

Have thoughts about how to make things better? Don't wait for someone to ask you what you think. Be bold and declare what you think should be done. The traditional fixers have a lot of other challenges to tackle. Most of them would be relieved to have you solve the issue.

Do your research

The more you know about your organization, the better positioned you will be to make change happen. Pay attention.

Build your network

Strive to get to know people throughout your organization. They can help you understand organizational dynamics, and, importantly, they may have the power to solve your problems.

Encourage future leaders

Kraemer notes that when you encourage colleagues to express their leadership potential, you are making both them and your organization stronger. You are also building allies who may be able to help you in the future.

Are you frustrated about what's not working in your organization? Name the problem. Build a coalition. Demand something better. Define what "better" looks like. When you are told change is impossible, ask "why?" over and over again until you wear the other person down.

You don't need to be in charge of anything to make change happen. Many times, you just need to ask the right questions.

OWN THE LANGUAGE

From behind a two-way mirror, we observe a group of unrelated people brought together for a focus group. The discussion topic on the floor is how unfair it is for family members to be saddled with taxes on money or property passed down after a loved one dies. By listening carefully in these discussions, the clever focus group leader seizes on the idea to replace the term "inheritance tax" with "death tax" to create outrage and generate public support for changing the tax code on the transfer of wealth from one generation to another. Or at least that is the story we are led to believe in the 2018 movie *Vice*, a comedy-drama about the political life of former vice president Dick Cheney. Some of the real-life characters represented in the movie have taken issue with the so-called historical facts chronicled in the film and point out specifically that the term "death tax" was used as early as the 1920s.[1] But historical accuracy aside, the substitution of "death tax" for "inheritance tax" is an excellent lesson in the power of language to sway people toward a desired direction.

Using the power of language is a key strategy for those who are savvy at negotiating organizational politics. Words have power, and the way we name things can propel an idea forward or lead to its demise. Consider the following word and phrase pairs.

Temporary assistance to needy families versus *welfare*. The first suggests financial support for families in need. The second signals a pejorative distribution of resources to those who may not deserve them.

Universal healthcare versus *socialized medicine.* The first signals a commitment to providing healthcare to all. The second suggests a practice at odds with US capitalism.

Poor versus *low-income.* The word "poor" can seem harsh and pitiful, while "low income" seems more objective and less emotional.

Torture versus *enhanced interrogation techniques:* Torture is inhumane and morally wrong, but many people find it hard to argue against getting to the truth by sophisticated question asking.

Social Security versus *entitlement programs.* Many of those who have paid into the Social Security program see the benefits of ensuring the economic stability of older community members. Those who oppose the program describe it as a mechanism of redistributing dollars to those who do not deserve them.

School vouchers versus *school choice.* The term "school vouchers" suggests the government is giving taxpayer money to those who want to send their children to private schools, while "school choice" suggests every family has a right to select a school that is right for them.

Victim versus *survivor.* The use of the word "survivor" changes the power dynamics of a criminal situation and empowers and affirms the individual who has been harmed in some way.

Perpetrator versus *respondent.* The word "perpetrator" suggests guilt, while "respondent" is a more neutral term meant to suggest that an individual is simply being called to account for an accusation.

Layoffs versus *rightsizing.* In one of the most disingenuous uses of language, corporations and the consultants they hired introduced the phrase "rightsizing" to suggest that mass terminations were simply a neutral business move.

Certainly, one of the most politically polarizing uses of language occurs in the abortion arena, where those who oppose the procedure declare themselves to be pro-life, while those who support the right to terminate a pregnancy describe themselves as pro-choice.

We even see the power of language at certain coffee establishments where small coffees are called "tall."

Language can also be manipulated by playing to the limited vocabulary of certain audiences. While the veracity of the reporting on Florida senator George Smathers's use of campaign rhetoric in the 1950s has been challenged, he was reputed to have called his opponent, Claude Pepper, a "shameless *extrovert*" (which sounds an awful lot like "pervert") and criticized him for habitually practicing "*celibacy*" before his marriage and having a sister who was a "*thespian*" (to be intentionally confused with "lesbian") "in wicked New York."[2]

True or not, this story made its way into political folklore as an example of the power of using language to influence political opinions. The tactic of using the right words can be effectively applied in workplace settings as well.

Imagine trying to generate commitment to examine corporate pay practices. Instead of asking senior leaders to increase pay for women, they might be asked about their commitment to "pay parity." A reduction in available parking spaces could be framed as an "environmental commitment strategy." Reducing the employer contribution to employee health insurance premiums might be described as a new "cost-sharing partnership."

Language has the power to provoke, upset, energize, and mobilize. It can also be used to calm people down. In some cases, language can be used to intentionally distract or confuse audiences. When launching an initiative, planning a bold move, assembling a committee, or responding to an internal or external threat, the name the effort is given matters. Those who are politically savvy decide in advance how they want their initiative to be received and build a name designed to move audiences to the appropriate emotion.

Interested in moving an idea forward? Think about how language will affect how others receive it. Using words and concepts aligned with their personal values will almost always increase their level of receptivity and the likelihood of you achieving the result you are after.

MIMIC THEIR MOVES

Have you ever met someone and immediately felt like you clicked with them? This sometimes happens quite naturally when two people have a lot in common, but it also occurs when the other person is being intentional in their engagement with you and quite deliberately using the technique of human mirroring. Mirroring occurs when one person imitates the tone of voice, emotion, or gestures of another. This act of behaving like the other can lead to a sense of rapport and connection. We think to ourselves, *We are acting alike, so we must be alike,* and we assume that our interests and attitudes must be aligned.[1] When people act like we do, we tend to trust them more because they give us a sense of safety and belonging.[2]

While some mirroring behavior is unconscious—you yawn, I yawn; you greet me warmly, I smile in return; you express enthusiasm for an idea, I get excited as well; you use curse words, I drop an f-bomb to show solidarity—mirroring can be practiced in a more calculated and strategic way. If you watch especially politically savvy players engage with others, you will see many of them practice human mirroring. As their conversation partner leans forward, they lean forward. As their conversation partner uses hand gestures to illustrate points, they become more physically animated as well.[3]

Mirroring can also be used to change behavior. Because most of us have a need to belong, we want to behave in ways that lead us to be accepted by others. You may notice that if you express anger and agitation when talking to a health insurance company representative, he may lower his voice and express kind remorse that your prescription card is not working. The goal here is to encourage you. the person on the other end of the phone line, to mirror calmness and civility. Hostage negotiators and SWAT team members use this tactic as well.[4]

When we think of the human mirroring effect, we tend to think of physical gestures and tones of voice, but we can also employ this technique by paying attention to the language that others use as well as their orientation toward decision-making, problem solving, idea generation, and change. A number of models have been advanced for this, and many of them draw upon research from David Keirsey and Marilyn Bates, who wrote *Please Understand Me* in 1978. Keirsey and Bates have asserted that people can be categorized into one of four archetypes: rational, guardian, artisan, and idealist.[5] Keirsey expanded on this work, publishing *Please Understand Me II* twenty years later.[6] Keirsey and Bates's original model was extended by Dawn Markova and Angie McArthur, who used the slightly more relatable typologies of analytical, procedural, innovative, and relational in their book, *Collaborative Intelligence: Thinking with People Who Think Differently.*[7] Let's consider each one.

Analytical types are focused on results and see themselves as possessing ingenuity and willpower. They like facts and logic and are highly motivated by the ability to get things done. Efficiency is important to them, and they strive to solve problems because they like to see progress. Connecting with these individuals requires being prepared, getting to the point, providing executive summaries, and talking about outcomes. When thinking about this archetype, Keirsey invites us to imagine field marshals, inventors, architects, and masterminds.[8]

Their energy zappers: Small talk. Inefficiency. Consensus-building activities.

Words to engage with them: "Bottom line." "Hit our targets." "Performance goals." "Shareholder value."

Procedure-oriented individuals value stability, reliability, service, and following the rules. They like detailed plans and plenty of time to consider the implications of a proposed plan of action. They are especially concerned about process, procedure, and tactics. Keirsey classifies people in this category as supervisors, inspectors, providers, and protectors.[9] When engaging with a person who has this orientation, it is wise to be prepared with historical information and ample data and to offer proof that what you are proposing is legal, ethical, and in conformance with past precedent.

Their energy zappers: Vague proposals, compressed deadlines for decision-making, and unusual ideas.

Words to engage with them: "Our policy allows for this." "There is legal precedent." "Our peers are already using this approach."

Innovative types are creative and fascinated by novelty, possibilities, the future, and the big picture. They like to be bold, delight in being audacious, and strive to be unique and the first ever to do something. Keirsey describes these people as promoters, performers, crafters, and composers.[10]

Their energy zappers: Procedures and routine.

Words to engage with them: "National model." "First out of the gate." "First ever."

Relationship-oriented people value community building, collaboration, relationships, forging connections, harmony, consensus, and demonstrating kindness. They stress the importance of teamwork, organizational morale, developing people, and minimizing conflict. Teachers, counselors, champions, and healers are among those whom Keirsey finds most concerned about the people of an organization.[11]

Their energy zappers: Conflict, rigidity, divisive organizational politics.

Words to engage them: "Community." "Values." "We have consensus on this." "Everyone agrees."

Table 1 offers a quick comparison of each personality type.

Table 1: How to connect with different workstyles

WORK STYLE	WHAT THEY VALUE	ENERGIZERS	ENERGY ZAPPERS
ANALYTICAL	Getting things done	Solving problems	Inefficiency
PROCEDURAL	Consistency	Well-documented protocols	Ambiguity
INNOVATIVE	Novelty, innovation	Being first	Routine
RELATIONAL	Harmony, community	Consensus	Discord

Source: Adapted from Markova, D., & McArthur, A. (2015). *Collaborative Intelligence.* New York: Random House.

With these archetypes in mind, let's consider how you might advance two very different proposals. The first is to secure support to build sleeping rooms and offer thirty-minute daily rest breaks to all employees; the second is to create buy-in for reducing your workforce by 10 percent. Let's consider how we might approach each personality archetype to get the results we want.

To move the sleeping rooms and thirty-minute rest breaks idea forward, we might consider the following:

Analytical. "Studies have shown that thirty minutes of rest can increase afternoon productivity by forty percent."

Procedural. "Twenty percent of comparably sized organizations offer nap rooms, and our legal counsel is supportive. Here is a detailed plan for how we might implement this."

Innovative. "We could be the first accounting firm in the nation to offer this research-based strategy for increasing both accuracy and productivity."

Relational. "Offering thirty-minute recharge breaks would reduce tension and minimize stress and exhaustion-related conflict."

To create buy-in for reducing 10 percent of your workforce as a strategy to free up cash for technology investments, you might consider the following talking points:

Analytical. "Our stockholder value will increase significantly, and this move will position us as one of the nation's most cost-effective service providers."

Procedural. "We will base our layoff decisions on performance evaluation scores, followed by years of service. Here is a detailed plan to guide us through the process."

Innovative. "Once we have more liquidity, we will be able to invest in new artificial intelligence solutions that will make us even more responsive to our customers."

Relational. "We are going to be very respectful as we move through this process. We have lined up outplacement counselors, and we are prepared to offer general severance packages and six months of health insurance for all those affected by these layoffs."

If you are trying to move an idea forward or are charged with accomplishing a major initiative, you will want to be sure you engage each of these types to polish your idea and move it from concept to execution. Each personality type will share with you the strengths and pitfalls of your approach and give you an opportunity to refine it. Developing different communication approaches for each work style may be a necessary strategy for moving your plan forward.

While crafting messages based on the receiver's personality style and personal values is important when trying to move controversial projects forward, these strategies can also be used in routine day-to-day conversations. Expressing interest in what matters most to others and speaking in a language that is aligned with their own can position you as an ally rather than an adversary. When others perceive that we get them, it is so much easier to work with them effectively

HOW TO COMPLAIN

Like anyone in a leadership position, I have received my fair share of angry complaints during my career, but two in particular stand out for me. One came from an employment applicant who had hoped to land a part-time teaching position with my university. In his email, which was copied to a parade of others, the writer said he was both surprised and angered to have been rejected for the role. He noted that cronyism and age discrimination were at play and demanded that the hiring manager and several others be terminated for their incompetence.

Fair process is important to me, so I looked into the situation to determine if there was anything to the conspiracy he described. In doing so, I learned that the hiring department had simply canceled the search. He wasn't hired, and neither was anyone else. I sent our angry correspondent a brief message explaining all of that and expressing regret that we had inconvenienced him. The applicant—clearly needing to get in the last word—responded with a series of messages sent to people across the university condemning my writing skills, integrity, and personal character.

The second message came late at night from a senior faculty member who was furious about what he perceived to be an "arbitrary" application of university policy. In a series of tersely worded sentences, the writer let me know how misguided the university and my staff were for failing to understand his needs. I responded by expressing regret at his frustration and offering a couple of options to get him what he wanted, though not necessarily in the way he wanted it.

The following morning, I received an even angrier message from the faculty member that was copied to multiple parties, informing me that my solutions were unacceptable and, like the first writer I mentioned, offering several sentences that questioned my general competence and integrity.

I must say, for the record, that I believe in being responsive even to people who appear to lack manners or impulse control, but there is never any joy in helping a person who writes nasty-grams— and that is what makes the angry approach so misguided. I am constantly surprised that people compromise the likelihood of getting what they want by alienating the very people who might be in a position to help them. It is normal to want to express frustration and demand justice when we feel we have been wronged. We might want to lash out, punish, and spread the word about how badly we have been treated. But having seen the difference in outcomes that result from complaining well versus complaining poorly, I know for certain that taking a more measured approach tends to yield better results.

Do you have a grievance to air? Here are some tips to consider:

Gather your facts. Make it easy to research and resolve your concerns. When did this bad thing happen? Who gave you information and/or misinformation? What, exactly, were you told?

Be brief. You are requesting assistance to fix something, not writing a novel. Multipage missives are rarely effective, so get to the point quickly in your complaint and keep your message short.

Ask for help. Do it politely: "I'm hoping you can help me understand" is often a good way to start.

Be curious, not furious. Express surprise and curiosity rather than outrage about your situation. Assume goodwill rather than intentional malice.

Don't make things worse by hurling insults. Phrases like "classic bureaucratic incompetence," "overpaid clerk," and "oppressive corporate overlords" are not generally helpful.

Ask for what you want. Be specific about your desired remedy.

Target your message. While sending a complaint to multiple people might seem like a smart strategy, it usually backfires. When seven people receive a complaint, each assumes the other six will handle it.

Don't start by going public. We have all heard stories about people who had wrongs righted after posting something embarrassing on social media platforms,[1] but this may not be a strategic approach. Embarrassing an employer or service provider may not engender a willingness to deal with your grievance. While turning to social media as a first step may move the entity that has wronged you to quicker action, it does not signal that you are a reasonable person. While some people may disagree, I think it is prudent to reserve social-media rants for situations in which all other avenues have been exhausted.

Begin in the right place. Rather than target your complaint to the head of the organization, send your concern to the person best positioned to handle it. Senior executives get hundreds of messages each day, so starting at the top of the organizational chart is likely to delay a possible remedy.

Be judicious in copying the next level up. It is tempting to punish people who have wronged us by making sure their supervisors know of their "incompetence." However, you don't need to create trouble or embarrassment. If the first level won't or can't help you, then travel up the chain but give people a chance to fix your problem.

Don't think threatening legal action will make things move faster. Sure, go ahead—hire a lawyer if you want. But you might be better off by first trying to resolve things more cheaply and quickly without the lawyers involved. Once you "go legal," there will be fewer people to resolve your issue, and reaching a resolution will generally take longer.

If you have managed your complaint well and your concern has been resolved, it will be time for you to express appreciation. Yes, I know you shouldn't have to take the time to thank someone who originally did you wrong, but it feels good to be thanked. When we express kindness to others, they are more likely to seek additional opportunities to make things right for the next person who has a problem—and that may benefit us again in the future.

Furthermore—and this is important—closing the loop well enables you to redefine your relationship with the person who initially caused you harm. The two of you are now partners rather than adversaries, and should you need assistance or want to engage in the future, you may have an advocate rather than an opponent.

MANAGE YOUR MEETINGS

No book about organizational politics would be complete without a chapter on navigating meetings, because this is where so many political moves are on clear display. We love to complain about meetings, don't we? We grumble about unclear or even secret agendas, having to jockey for airtime, annoying coworkers who dominate conversations, tiresome skirmishes between rivals and factions, and the need to offer moral support to colleagues whose good ideas are routinely shot down for political reasons. The good news is that pointless, unproductive, and politically charged meetings can be transformed into more meaningful interactions that yield actual results. Doing so starts with attending to the structure of our gatherings and being intentional about elevating the voices that are typically muffled or silenced.

Amplifying diverse voices is not a radical idea; it is, after all, a fundamental strategy for fostering a sense of inclusion.[1] But giving others a voice does more than foster a sense of belonging; it leads to greater innovation and more strategic decision-making.[2] When the usual suspects do all the talking and only the loud voices drive conversations, we miss opportunities for considering better options. So if you are committed to better meetings, consider the dynamics at the current meetings you are attending. Who is talking? Who is not listening? Who can't seem to break into the conversation? Most importantly, are you committed to doing something about it? If you are, here are some strategies to consider.

Respect different thinking styles

We all have different ways of thinking and processing information. Some people think on the fly and rarely know what they are going to say until the words have emerged from their mouths. They think by talking. Others need time to consider possibilities and are uncomfortable voicing opinions or sharing ideas without time for considered reflection. To honor this and to ensure that both introverted and extroverted thinkers are positioned to be full meeting participants, send out meeting agendas and information in advance.

Track who's talking

A group called Gender Avenger created an app called "Are Men Talking Too Much?" that can be used to track gender differences in airtime in a fairly discreet manner.[3] For more specific information about which meeting members are consuming the most airtime, you can use a more precise and low-tech approach. At the beginning of some of my meetings, I write down everyone's name and make tick marks as each person speaks. In doing so, I have confirmed that in many gatherings, a couple of the attendees tend to dominate the conversation, and at least 25 percent say nothing at all. To be fully transparent, I must confess that I was disappointed to see an excessive number of tick marks by my own name when I first started this tracking process. Fortunately, this self-monitoring strategy has motivated me to be more judicious about when to share my thoughts and when to create space for others to express theirs.

Establish group agreements

In my experience, proposals to create meeting ground rules are generally met with heavy sighs and eye rolling. The process strikes many as overly formal and even juvenile, but those who stick with it tend to report that cocreating commitments about how to work together can be a powerful expression of values that significantly improves meeting dynamics. To reduce cynicism, refer to these rules as "working agreements" or "group agreements" rather than using the often polarizing "ground rules" language. These agreements do not have to be complex and may include commitments regarding raising hands to speak, promises not to revisit items that have already been decided, calling out interrupters and credit stealers, and having the meeting facilitator give each person an opportunity to weigh in before those who have already spoken are allowed to speak again. A little awkward? Yes. Effective? Absolutely.

The beauty of group agreements is that they create a useful structure for assessing the effectiveness of gatherings. Many high-performing groups make it a practice to engage in debriefings after their meetings. Did we follow our group agreements? Did we stay on track? Who talked, and who did not? Did each of us feel heard? Did we make necessary decisions? Was this gathering a good use of time?

Rotate meeting leadership

Too often the person with the most organizational power leads meetings. This creates two key challenges. First, it is hard to be both a meeting facilitator and a full participant; few of us can balance both roles effectively. Second, when the person with power expresses an opinion, it can discourage those with conflicting points of view to challenge the idea on the table. Consider rotating meeting leadership responsibilities to encourage broader participation and build meeting facilitation muscles among all team members.

Use creative input gathering

Liberating Structures are a collection of meeting tools designed to harness the intelligence of groups. One of my favorite tools is called 1-2-4-All. In this technique, a question is posed to the group, and each person is given a few minutes to write down their thoughts. That is "one." Next, meeting participants pair up to discuss what they have written. This is "two." Next, two pairs get together to engage in a similar process. That is "four." Finally, everyone comes back together to hear from several sets of four. That is the "all." This process supports hearing from individuals and allows multiple approaches to be refined in a supportive manner.

Manage interruptions

Maintaining the floor when other meeting participants are loud, energetic, and opinionated can be challenging, so make sure that everyone knows how to manage chronic interrupters. Veronica Rueckert shares some especially artful techniques in her book *Outspoken: Why Women's Voices Get Silenced and How to Set Them Free*.[4] I especially like the "snapback," which involves leaning forward, holding up a single finger in the general direction of the interrupter, and saying, "I want to finish this thought." When that fails, Rueckert recommends the more pointed "nuclear option": "Carl, you interrupted me. Let me pick up . . . " In virtual meeting settings, it can be useful to designate one participant as the "silencer" who has the power to mute an attendee who won't stop talking.

Enlist allies

Challenging floor hogs and interrupters can seem or even be risky for those without much power, so it can be strategic to engage allies in advance. This might take the form of asking a colleague to be on the lookout for interruptions and to call them out: "Hey, Ramone was in the middle of making a point." Allies can also create room for a quiet voice to jump in. "We haven't heard from Jacqui yet. Let's get her thoughts before we move on." They can also call out the credit stealers: "I like the way you are building on Tolgar's idea."

Call out bullies

Few things chill productive conversation more than aggressive behavior and personal attacks. While protocols for civil engagement should be in your group agreements, if they do not exist, make it a practice to call out rude and intimidating behavior. "Marla, seriously?" or "Javier, it's fine to disagree, but Clarise is not an idiot." Silence emboldens bullies. Break their cycle of abuse by calling it out and making their bad behavior obvious.

Allow for after-meeting input

Even when we make it safe for all meeting members to speak up, we may notice that some colleagues find it difficult to share their perspectives. Given this, it can be valuable to create a routine for collecting feedback and ideas after the meeting concludes. This, of course, needs to be an option provided to everyone. When an issue is not time-sensitive, consider building in a post-meeting input process. "Thank you for sharing your perspectives today. If you have additional thoughts, send me an email by Tuesday, and I'll include your input in the meeting minutes."

Consider that you might be the problem

I recently worked with an executive who was struggling with an underperforming leadership team. When detailing his challenges, he complained that despite the members' expertise and experience, none of them introduced new ideas or proposed solutions. He expressed frustration that he was forced to do all of the thinking. As I sat in the background for one of his meetings, the cause of his frustration quickly became obvious. He dominated the conversation, answered questions that others could have easily tackled, and talked over those who attempted to share a different point of view. He had unwittingly trained them not to speak up. Annoyed that others aren't talking? Try keeping your mouth shut for a while.

DETERMINE WHETHER THE PROBLEM COMES FROM SLACKERS OR STRUCTURE

Conversations about organizational politics can be more interesting and amusing when we talk about unintended workplace phenomena and the various laws, principles, and effects that researchers use to name them. You probably know many of them. Most of us are well versed on the Peter principle, the tendency for people in organizations to rise to their level of incompetence.[1] So when an associate director is promoted to a director role and flounders, we often say, "That's the Peter principle in action."

Many of us are also familiar with Parkinson's law, the propensity of work to fill the time available for its completion.[2] Anyone who has had to submit a report on deadline, grade exams, or design a presentation knows that work rarely gets completed before its due date.

The Dunning-Kruger effect is one of my favorite phenomena because it is useful to have a name for why it is that smart and highly talented people often underestimate their abilities, while incompetent people believe themselves to be unusually clever and effective.[3] The research that suggests men overestimate their abilities while women underestimate theirs is especially interesting.[4] Even more fascinating, but also troubling, is that individuals with a higher socioeconomic status are more overconfident than those with a lower socioeconomic status.[5]

Fewer of us are aware of Goodhart's law, which asserts that when a measure becomes a target, it ceases to be a good measure.[6] For example, when we evaluate others based on a focused outcome such as donor requests made, the percentage of math students who pass a course, or the number of loan applications reviewed, people inevitably learn to hit the target by reducing quality. Fundraising professionals may schedule visits to prospects who lack the means to make sizable philanthropic gifts, teachers may make math exams too easy, and loan officers may fail to give full consideration to mortgage applicants with shaky credit histories because gathering additional documentation would take too much time.

One phenomenon that is particularly ubiquitous in almost all work and community organization settings is the Ringelmann effect. This is the tendency for individual members of a group to become less productive as the size of their group increases.[7] The phenomenon got its name in the early twentieth century when French agricultural engineer Max Ringelmann had a group of people engage in a game of tug of war—first as individuals and then again as members of a team. Ringelmann discovered that twice as many people does not lead to twice as much effort. In fact, as the number of team members increased, individual contributions tended to decline.

You have probably noticed this and wondered why it often seems impossible to get anything done unless you do it yourself. You may have silently or even publicly cursed your colleagues for being lazy or incompetent and uttered phrases like "never again" after serving on a particularly hellacious group project. According to Ringelmann's research, it might be time to lighten up and consider that you have created the problem that is frustrating you.

Ringelmann initially speculated that more participants made coordination more challenging, and that certainly makes sense, but his later experiments showed something quite different. He eventually concluded that individuals in large groups fail to exert exceptional effort in order to save their energy for activities that will lead them to be individually recognized. We will go all out when all eyes are on us, but we tend to take it easy when we think our colleagues can do the hard work, when we will not be held accountable for the eventual outcome, when we suspect our effort is not truly necessary, or when we anticipate that our time and energy will not be appropriately rewarded.

How does the Ringelmann effect reveal itself in various settings? Examples seem almost endless, but let's consider three common scenarios.

Example 1. You assembled a ten-person team of high-powered technical experts to lead a major information technology project. They scoped out the project, offered reasonable budget expectations, and delivered a plan to hit the requested deadline. Then the group moved the deadline again and again, unable to sustain the intensity and focus needed to move the project to completion.

Example 2. Wanting to demonstrate a commitment to "volunteer voice" and ensure that key stakeholder groups were represented in the search for a new nonprofit executive director, the board president invited fifteen people to participate on the search committee. Everyone showed up for the initial meeting, but when it came to doing real work, only the committee co-chairs expended much effort.

Example 3. An especially bright and dynamic junior consultant who is considering joining your firm mentioned her interest in partnering with a high-profile senior partner who, unknown to her, has a reputation for suggesting that strategy conversations occur over drinks in his hotel room.

Because this is widely known in the firm, you don't say anything, knowing you can count on the other junior consultants to give her the warning she needs.

There is certainly a difference between being an absentee committee member and being complicit in allowing sexual misconduct to go unchecked, but we can point to the Ringelmann effect to understand each behavior. Assuming that there are plenty of others to do the heavy lifting minimizes a sense of personal accountability. When we think we can count on others to do the necessary work, or at least not be personally blamed for it not getting done, it is easy to tell ourselves that our personal disengagement will not be noticed.

Given the damage that can occur to others, our organizations, and even our own careers when the Ringelmann effect reveals itself, how can we minimize its occurrence? There are a number of strategies we can employ, and here are a few to consider.

Keep teams small

Teams of three to five make it hard for slackers to hide. If broader stakeholder representation is necessary, let a bigger advisory team offer input to a small group tasked with doing the real work.

Establish working agreements early on

Before work begins, seek agreement on how group members will work together. Establish who will do what, develop accountability measures, and decide how members will be informed when they are and are not meeting expectations.

Let group members play to their strengths and involve them only when they are needed

We all struggle when we don't like the work that has been

handed to us or worry about our capacity to deliver on it. We should let those with project management expertise create the month-by-month plans. Ask those who enjoy research to do the background work. Task the communicators with designing presentations. Be explicit that you are counting on the well connected to build behind-the-scenes support. Finally, invite the strongest presenters to do the public speaking.

Acknowledge work styles when assigning roles and responsibilities

Most of us come to workgroups or project teams with varied talents. Some of us have a knack for identifying challenges, others are adept at proposing solutions, and some are strong at implementing recommendations, while there always seems to be at least one member of any group prepared to point out the flaws in any approach. Rather than being annoyed that everyone is not obviously pulling in the same direction in the same way, seek to understand where the tension is coming from. *The Innovative Team* authors Chris Grivas and Gerald J. Puccio argue that innovation requires us to understand and embrace varied working and thinking styles, and they report that when it comes to working in teams, most of us can be classified as one of four work roles: clarifiers, ideators, developers, or implementers.[8] Each plays an important role in moving work from concept to completion. Given this, we should invite the clarifiers to define the challenge, the ideators to generate possibilities, the developers to refine options, and the implementers to move ideas from concept to action.

Regularly evaluate both group and individual progress

Recognize team members who honor their commitments and offer support to team members who are not meeting performance deadlines or targets. Recognize that underperformers may not be intentionally shirking their responsibilities; they may simply be ill-equipped to deliver what is expected.

Recognize both team and individual contributions

The promise of individual recognition creates greater incentives for members to be full contributors. To support this, individual roles and responsibilities must be clearly defined.

Periodically ask each group member to report on their contributions and to recognize the contributions of others

Knowing that peers will be evaluating us has a way of moving us to action and makes our colleagues more comfortable calling us out if we fail to honor our commitments.[9]

The strategies described thus far are appropriate for minimizing the Ringelmann effect in day-to-day work and special project teams, but are certain strategies particularly effective in preventing or at least reducing sexual misconduct or other forms of inappropriate workplace conduct? Organizations should focus on two strategies. First, *establish community commitments* and then post them publicly and review them regularly. Describe what is expected rather than what is discouraged while being clear that protecting our colleagues is a shared responsibility. Next, *periodically ask each team member to report on their contributions toward building a healthy culture and to recognize the contributions of their colleagues.* Make it clear that we are all responsible for creating safe working and learning environments and invite each person to note the varied ways they have contributed to this shared commitment.

Politics and organizational dynamics can often impede our ability to get things done in almost any setting, and when the Ringelmann effect takes hold, making progress can seem almost impossible. Being attentive to structure and group dynamics, and employing some of the strategies described here, can increase organizational effectiveness and project success, all while creating the kind of culture necessary for members to be both safe and productive.

SURVIVING
TRANSITIONS

FIGURE OUT WHAT THEY WANT

Whenever there is a change in leadership in an organization, at least a few people get nervous. Will the new person in charge think I'm competent? Will the current balance of power and status be disrupted? Most importantly, will I survive in the new world order? Many people do just fine when a new leader takes over, but those who do not often have something in common: they fail to manage up. That is the practice of engaging those above you in the organizational food chain in the way they prefer to be engaged and acting in alignment with their priorities. Managing up differs from sucking up in that it requires adapting rather than selling your soul. Should you find yourself reporting to someone new or even failing to thrive with someone you have reported to for some time, consider the following questions:

Who clicks with the leader? Who are the leader's go-to people or confidants? What do those people do, and why does it seem to work for them?

What matters most to the leader? Does he want to be known as a reformer or as a leader committed to order, stability, and accountability? Is she interested in being known as an innovator? Does he need to be popular? Does she value harmony? Once you figure that out, how can you frame your ideas in ways that will resonate with those priorities?

How does the new leader want to receive information from you? One person I know assumed that because her new boss responded to email messages with one-sentence answers, he wanted her to write equally brief messages. It turned out that he actually wanted details but did not have the time to craft lengthy responses. Another person drove his supervisor crazy by cranking out multi-issue novellas instead of the brief, to-the-point messages that he preferred. When in doubt, ask.

How much information are you expected to provide? Does the new leader want to know everything that's going on, or expect reports on areas of strategic importance only? What is the preferred format for sharing that information? Orally? In writing? Bullet points? With plenty of details? Again, asking is better than guessing. Find out the preferred way of providing information.

What is the expected meeting protocol? Are you meant to talk, or are you meant to listen? If only some people are meant to talk, are you one of them?

Given the ever-shorter tenures of organizational leaders, many of us experience leadership shifts on a regular basis and are constantly having to adapt to new styles and preferences. While revolving-door leadership is not a new phenomenon, the pace of the twirling seems to have ticked up recently, and this requires those who are expected to welcome new leaders to be on constant alert for clues about what the new people want and expect.

It did not surprise me that a hot topic of conversation at a conference I attended recently was focused on how to make sense of new leaders' styles and unspoken expectations. Here are just a few of the comments that were shared:

"The last CEO wanted immediate updates on anything controversial, but the new one yelled at me for sending him an email marked 'Alert' on a Saturday."

"She hasn't said anything directly, but the way she looked me up and down tells me that she doesn't believe dresses should be sleeveless."

"She gave me her personal phone number but failed to tell me I am never supposed to use it."

"It would have been helpful for him to tell me up front that he thinks using Calibri font makes his messages look too casual."

"I asked several people for feedback and was castigated for 'breaking rank' by asking people at higher levels to comment on my proposal. I go to happy hour with most of these people regularly, but I guess I'm not supposed to communicate with them at work."

Getting burned for breaking rules we don't know exist can be unnerving and demoralizing, and I think most of us agree that it would be helpful and far more efficient for new leaders to simply publish their list of likes and dislikes and to be explicit about actions and behaviors that can lead one to be shunned or even dismissed. Learning what is annoying or unacceptable by trial (by fire) and error is not terribly effective or energizing.

If you are a new leader, think about your preferred protocols and take some time to document them. If you are the one welcoming the new leader, be prepared with some questions:

What is your preferred mode of receiving information? Do you prefer bulleted lists, executive summaries, or comprehensive reports? Does your answer change depending on the topic?

How do you want to hear from me? Written reports? Text messages? Scheduled meetings? Drop-in conversations?

What do you want to hear from me? Performance updates? Current challenges? Emerging trends? Organizational gossip?

What topics do you consider urgent, and which can wait for a more routine update? How late is too late for a call or message from me?

Is there a dress code we should know about? Do your expectations for in the office differ from what I should consider for external meetings?

Do you have a preferred style for written communication? Do you have a preferred font? What is your position on Oxford commas?

How would you like me to interact in meetings? Should I speak up if I have an idea or concern, or would you prefer me to discuss this with you in private?

The more you understand your new manager's preferences, the more you can create a sense of connection. That, in turn, leads to trust. And that, in turn, leads to a bit more job security.

WATCH YOUR BACK WHEN YOU'RE IN CHARGE

Congratulations—you're in charge! After years of taking orders, you now get to issue them. You will have the freedom to make your own plans, set your own direction, and surround yourself with people who share your work ethic and point of view. Life is good! The only problem? None of this will actually be true.

It can be exhilarating to be tapped for a leadership role, but while you may consider yourself to be the boss now, unless you own your company, there will still be a boss above you. That means you will have to satisfy both those above you and those below you on the organizational chart—and that could prove to be a mighty tight squeeze. While it is theoretically possible that you will have flexibility to choose who works with you, you are more likely to face barriers when it comes to picking and choosing. It's quite likely you'll be stuck with the team you inherit, and it will be up to you to make that team work.

I share this news not to depress you but to prepare you. New leaders are often surprised and disappointed by the realities of their situations, so if you're about to move into a leadership role or are considering one in the future, here are a few things you should know.

You may not have been the people's choice

It is quite possible that you were selected against the advice and wishes of the people who now report to you.

They may have supported another candidate or simply wanted anyone but you. The fact that you are in charge now may be a disappointment to them, and it is likely they will invest a considerable amount of time prowling for evidence to prove that you are the wrong person for the role. Endeavor not to express exasperation when your qualifications are debated within earshot.

The other finalist now reports to you, and he's not happy

The person who wanted your job even more than you did is reminded on a basis daily that you got the role he wanted. While he may congratulate you in public, he is likely to be bitter and sarcastic and may actively undermine you. Watch your back and by no means take him to coffee to explain how you appreciate that the situation is difficult; that will just make him feel worse.

You may be lonely

If you were promoted from within, the people you used to count as friends and happy-hour companions now report to you, and they know you are no longer one of them. While there might be occasional lunch gatherings, the sense of camaraderie you previously enjoyed is likely to dissipate. Your information sources will likely dry up, and you will need to find a new support network. This will feel sad and hard.

Being the boss does not mean you get to be bossy

It is easy to spot a newbie boss. She is the one who makes unreasonable requests, demands detailed updates, and micromanages every project. More seasoned leaders actually pay attention to the research on employee motivation and know that most of us are inspired by having a strong sense of purpose, a fair amount of autonomy, and the ability to demonstrate our personal strengths on a regular basis.[1] Savvy leaders seek to energize and inspire their people, not to torment and terrify them.

Your people are probably smarter than you are

Need something done? By all means ask for a finished product, but don't prescribe how every step of the process should look. Others probably have better ideas than you do. Don't get in their way.

Claim credit for other people's ideas at your peril

The minute you take credit for someone else's idea is the minute you will crush future demonstrations of creative or intellectual expression. Phrases like "I have a great team" are completely insufficient to demonstrate recognition and appreciation. You must utter people's names and thank them publicly and profusely.

Leadership is a series of tough conversations

Being in charge means you have to be honest and direct. That doesn't mean you have to be ruthless, however. Pick up a book like *Radical Candor*[2] or *Difficult Conversations*[3] to learn how to offer the gift of constructive feedback. While you're in reading mode, check out *Thanks for the Feedback*[4] for tips on how to accept feedback yourself.

When it comes to tough conversations, don't hesitate or dither, because nothing good comes from delaying what needs to be said. If you've got something to say, say it.

Demonstrating vulnerability will make you stronger, not weaker

So many of us think demonstrating vulnerability makes us seem weaker, but the courage to admit mistakes and missteps actually makes us stronger.[5] When we demonstrate vulnerability, we seem more human and real, and that makes us more relatable. It is far easier to forge an emotional connection with someone who is fallible than with someone who is perfect. If you fumble, own it.

Your best people are likely to leave—and that's okay

Good people leave. That's not an indictment of your leadership; it's just what happens when talented people are ready for something bigger. You can characterize the departures as betrayals and acts of abandonment, or you can pivot and express pride in your ability to launch outstanding people. It is helpful to have supportive allies on the outside, so don't be bitter when your best people venture off.

You will have to work harder than anyone else if you want to be taken seriously

If you dare to work less than those who report to you, you will be labeled as an entitled slacker. While you are allowed to establish boundaries, if you take more vacation than others in your group, come in later, or leave earlier, people will talk, and that talk will not be good. If you want a life outside of work, make sure everyone else in your organization has it first.

The move from one of the gang to the person in charge can be a bumpy journey, and the isolation that can come from leaving the pack is often surprising and disorienting. Missteps are easy to make, and you can be assured everyone will be taking notes when you stumble. Your motives will be questioned, your decisions will be challenged, and your personal integrity will be called into question—over and over again. If that sounds like something you can handle, you are ready for your new role.

OWN THE MESS YOU'VE INHERITED

A friend of mine recently accepted a big job in a new city. Before she began, she was excited. The man to whom she was to report was supportive, her would-be peers seemed both strategic and welcoming, and her new staff seemed genuinely excited about her arrival. The division seemed strong, the budget was reasonable, and the community in which she would live was described as welcoming. But within a few weeks of her arrival, she had a sinking feeling. At the end of her second month on the job, she knew she'd made a terrible mistake.

Her boss was affable but not that interested in her work or available to help. Her division peers were definitely strategic, but they also engaged in regular backbiting to curry favor with the senior vice president. The budget seemed large, but no one had mentioned upfront that it was insufficient to meet current obligations, much less to offer a margin for new investments. And her team members? While they were gracious and enthusiastic during her initial meetings, they were surly and cantankerous after she moved across the country to join them.

During a late-night conversation—one in which I could hear her pouring a few glasses of wine—we talked about her interview and site visit process. We sought to retrace her steps to understand how her assessment of the opportunity could have been so inaccurate. Our conclusion: she had been intentionally misled.

When she asked to meet with key work partners, the response was, "They are going a hundred miles a minute here, and you aren't our only finalist."

When she asked to meet with her division's director of finance during the final interview visit, he was put on her itinerary. Yet when it came time to meet, he was suddenly unavailable because of a family emergency.

She was never allowed to meet one-on-one with her team members. Every meeting included at least three people, thereby ensuring that no single individual could whisper in her ear about challenges she might face.

"You were played," I said after we reviewed the chain of events. "But there were obvious clues you missed because you wanted this job so much. The question now is: how will you move forward?"

My friend's experience felt familiar because I once faced a similar situation and learned some hard lessons about the dangers of excessive trust and optimism and the risks that come from failing to conduct due diligence. After once inheriting a mess, I behaved badly and spent an inordinate amount of time blaming my predecessor for leaving what I called "a bundle of lies," and I criticized the organization's leadership for handing me a rat's nest to untangle. I whined a lot and wasted a good amount of emotional energy on being angry. "Don't make the same mistake I made," I said to my friend. "Behave better than I did."

If you find that you have inherited a terrible mess, how should you move forward? You could take the lead of several US presidents and blame your predecessors, but that will make you seem weak and whiny.[1] It is not a strategy that works all that well, and it can also suggest that the colleagues you inherited were complicit in creating the mess you are now trying to clean up. You will need their support to turn things around, so alienating them will only delay your progress. Instead of complaining and being bitter, try the following strategies.

Speak as "us" rather than "you"

As the newcomer, you may be tempted to distance yourself from the mess, but don't. You now own it. Embrace your new organization and suggest that you are fully committed to turning things around.[2]

Be clear about your values

In times of crisis, your people need to know what matters to you and whether you view them as key to the organization's future. Be explicit about your expectations and what it will take to be successful when working with you.

Acknowledge what's working

It is important to be open about the many challenges facing the department. However, not everything is broken, so highlight points of pride.[3]

Share the numbers.

It is easy to dismiss the need for change when challenges are not obvious. Give your people the facts: "Our sales are down twelve percent," or "Fifteen percent of our clients say they would not recommend us," or "We have a two-million-dollar structural deficit." Defining the problem is a key first step in solving it.

Describe the future you imagine

Articulating a compelling vision offers a path forward and signals your optimism that things will eventually improve.

Don't go it alone. As quickly as possible, determine who on your team is hungry and who might be helpful, because you will need both phenotypes to master your mess. The hungry will work hard to make a name for themselves during the turnaround, and the helpful will be instrumental in providing the quiet, behind-the-scenes support that you will need to move things forward.

Embrace your mess as an opportunity

A sense of crisis can be a powerful bonding experience and can build long-term optimism and confidence by enabling organizational members to believe "We got through that; we can get through this."[4]

While it can be exhilarating to turn around a struggling organization, it is typically demoralizing to be delivered such a challenge without warning. There are usually obvious signs in the hiring process that all is not well, but we may miss or dismiss them when we want a position too much. If you are denied information or meeting opportunities during the search process, be prepared for an unhappy set of surprises once you arrive. It is good to be excited about a new job opportunity, but it is far better to be skeptical. Don't accept a new role until all of your questions have been answered.

BEWARE OF THE BOBBLEHEADS

You have finally gotten the key role you've always wanted. You are delighted that your team is filled with agreeable people who are completely aligned with your vision of the future. The road ahead looks rosy. Or does it? That all depends on how much you believe in the power of your brilliant ideas and whether you have surrounded yourself with strategic thinkers or a bunch of bobbleheads. Bobbleheads, are, of course, dolls with oversized heads that nod when poked. Only "yes" nods, of course. Bobbleheads never shake their heads to indicate a "no." You can find real-life bobbleheads inside many organizations.

The bobblehead phenomenon is described nicely in "The Seduction of the Leader in Higher Education," a highly useful monograph written by Patrick Sanaghan and Kimberly Eberbach. The piece, which is also applicable in settings outside of academia, describes the reasons leaders face real or metaphorical no-confidence votes, and key among them is the failure to obtain or consider dissenting points of view. The monograph's authors call this "seduction by sycophants." "If you aren't getting feedback that is challenging, being asked tough questions, or hearing contrary opinions," they write, "you can bet that seduction by sycophants is alive and well."[1]

If you are surrounded by sycophants who resemble bobbleheads, it is worth considering whether you attracted them or whether you created them. Have you made exces-

sive smiling and head nodding a job requirement?[2] Do you need to be the center of attention at all times? Have you signaled that you are not open to dissent by ousting those who disagree with you in public or even private?

Many bobbleheads are survivors by nature and will agree to absurd assignments and praise preposterous ideas to ensure their position and seat at the table. Some leaders surround themselves with these people because they tend to make life easy. They find it energizing to listen to their bobbleheads express enthusiasm for their plans and platforms. And they often make leaders feel super-humanly productive—invincible, even—as proposals sail through and thorny problems get resolved without messy debate. Nod, nod. Smile, smile. But, as many an ousted leader learns too late, bobbleheads can lead to their undoing. By making leaders feel smart, they eventually make them look stupid.

Sanaghan and Eberbach's monograph includes several smart ideas about encouraging others to speak the truth that leaders desperately need to hear. Some of their suggestions are harder to adopt than others, but one of the easiest is to develop a regular practice of inviting dissenting opinions by asking three safe questions:

"What argument would those who disagree with me make?"

"What biases of mine might be influencing my perspective?"

"Are there other solutions that would accommodate more agendas and be equally effective?"[3]

If you hold a leadership position and ask these three questions, you will signal that you expect rigorous thinking, not ego stroking and head nodding. It will also encourage your team to consider you flexible and open to hearing better ideas than the ones you create on your own. That will make your organization stronger and position you to keep your job a little longer.

If certain members of your team regularly fawn over your ideas, fall over themselves to compliment your "brilliant" deductions, and speak of your superior leadership skills, they are bobbleheads, and they will do nothing to make you better or stronger. In fact, they will simply contribute to a narrative that you surround yourself with suck-ups. It is critical that you make your expectations for honest and rigorous feedback clear and surround yourself with those with the courage to tell you what you need to know.

DON'T CONFUSE YOURSELF WITH A MESSIAH

The job market is always hot for turnaround magicians capable of lightning-speed transformation. If you have a record of turning around underperforming or completely broken organizations, you probably have your pick of opportunities. There is a shortage of people capable of transforming organizations in trouble, and you may be in serious demand if you have established a reputation as a fixer.

It is quite the ego boost to be considered a potential savior and tapped to deal with a challenge that seems intractable to others. Being asked to join an organization that really needs you can make you feel taller and stronger as you imagine yourself swooping in to perform acts of magic. But be careful. You may be good, but a messiah you are not. The minute your chest begins to swell is the point at which you should pause to consider whether you are destined to let arrogance interfere with your effectiveness. There is a strategic way to turn things around, and there is an egomaniacal way. Both can work in the short term, but only one approach is likely to lead to lasting results.

Let's begin by talking about the mode of operation employed by rookies and megalomaniacs. Believing themselves to be organizational messiahs, these individuals delight in identifying all that is wrong and all those who are incompetent. They ask no questions upon arrival because they assume no one else has anything of value to contribute. They use phrases like "legacy employees" and discount the value of institutional history. "I'm sure we'll figure things out," they respond when others suggest caution about tossing out people with strategic relationships or specialized knowledge.

While messiah-acting leaders often bring intelligence, focus, and fresh perspectives, they generally lack one ingredient critical for long-term success: the ability to create an environment in which people feel safe to perform, much less experiment and innovate. While these leaders may articulate a compelling vision of a better future, they tend to fail on execution because of their propensity to alienate the people they need to do the work. A sense of psychological safety is essential for intellectual and creative expression, and people who feel constantly belittled cannot deliver much for long.[1]

It is not surprising that those who imagine themselves to be organizational saviors tend to have short tenures. If you ask them why, they will say they accomplished the "disruption" they came to create, they need constant change, or they felt bogged down by the slow-moving and unsophisticated culture in which they landed.

Those answers will mostly be lies. Here's the truth: after making an initial splash, messiah-acting leaders run out of fuel— both resources and people's goodwill—and have to move on before things start crashing around them.

So if flashy, visionary, messiah-acting leaders are generally ineffective, what is the alternative?

The answer lies in selecting a leader who is inclined to honor and build upon past success—someone whose organizational philosophy is in line with appreciative inquiry, an approach developed by David L. Cooperrider and Suresh Srivastva.[2] Proponents and practitioners of appreciative inquiry seek to understand what is already working rather than what is so profoundly wrong. They assume the best of others and understand that inferior past performance may simply be a function of bad direction or misalignment of resources. They eschew the shock-and-awe, slash-and-burn tactics favored by the messiah-style leaders and instead attempt to leverage the talents already available within the organization. Because they exhibit respect and show appreciation, they are rewarded with cooperation and a willingness to try new ideas.

Certainly, a regular infusion of new people and ideas keeps organizations healthy and vibrant, but constant and wholesale churn makes it impossible to maintain momentum. Strategic leaders understand that structural and cultural issues can inhibit organizational performance as much as people with the wrong skills and attitudes can. That is why they attempt to improve the organizational ecosystem before instructing all the "legacy employees" to pack their boxes.

In his *Harvard Business Review* article "Leading the Team You Inherit," Michael D. Watkins urges new leaders to focus on people, alignment, operating models, and integration.[3] Following his advice, a new leader might ask:

- Do people in this organization have the necessary skills and attitude?
- Are they focused on the right activities?
- Are they working in ways that get things done?
- Do mutual interdependencies exist to support and leverage each person's success?
- Are they sharing the right kind and amount of information?
- Do people feel safe to offer ideas and express opinions?

If you are asked to turn around an organization, you will have a choice to make. You can position yourself as an organizational savior, or you can demonstrate a little humility and admit that you will need others in order to be successful.

NAVIGATING CHANGE

PAUSE BEFORE KILLING THE CUBS

I am not a fan of nature shows, but one night I joined my husband on the sofa to watch one that had him particularly riveted. The episode featured a male lion that had taken over a pride after the previous male had been killed in some kind of jungle melee. At first, I thought it looked like a good situation since the lion cubs would once again have two parents. But, oh, no, this was not a story with a happy ending. The new patriarch began killing the cubs. In a gruesome display of "I'll show you who's in charge around here," he punctured each of their furry little necks.

Why? Apparently there are many theories for this very common behavior, but one is that the male lions want to raise their own cubs, not someone else's, and they must dispense with existing cubs to create their own dynasties.[1] My husband turned to me and said, "Well, now we understand what's happening at work."

In certain industries, it is common for new organizational leaders to replace the members of their team soon after they arrive, and they offer several reasons for this. Some are legitimate, and some are not. Certainly, there are times when an existing team lacks the skill and vision necessary to be successful, but this is not always what drives the ousters. In some cases, there are mass firings to signal that it is a new day and to caution those who remain that what has worked in the past won't work anymore. In other cases, the ousters are motivated by questions about the potential loyalty of an inherited team and fear that their followers and alliances may impede progress in asserting organizational dominance. Metaphorical cubs are also killed when the new leader is charged with making profound changes, turning around an organization, or addressing deep cultural issues. Eliminating the people believed to have attachments to the old way of doing business is often seen as a necessary step toward transformation. While handpicking an entirely new leadership team may seem practical, there are often unintended consequences.

As I watched the cub-killing nature show, I thought back to a conversation I had with a university president several years ago after being contacted by a search firm looking for someone to do a "clean-up job." After a day with the people who would report to me, I had to agree that the organization was in need of a serious makeover. By about 4:00 p.m. or so, I had a game plan, and I shared it during my final meeting of the day with the president. It would be fair to say that the president did not find my insights brilliant. "I'm looking for someone to guide these people in the right direction, not to throw them into the street. I don't believe in slash and burn." That is not the reaction I was expecting, and as you might have already surmised, the flight home was long and lonely.

The dressing-down was painful, but I am indebted to this president for prompting me to examine the frequent rookie and lazy mistake of "killing the cubs" upon assuming a new leadership role. Wiser leaders appreciate that it is possible for loyalties to shift and that there can be danger in tossing out people with institutional knowledge and vital relationships that can facilitate success and actually expedite organizational transformation. Strategic leaders also know that creating fear and uncertainty through shock and awe–type leadership bloodbaths can destroy organizational morale and create profound distrust. Seasoned leaders know that taking time to accurately assess the suitability of their newly acquired "cubs" is smarter than immediately puncturing their necks to signify that it is a new day.

So, what if you are one of the "cubs" and need to weather a new leader? If you really want to stay, it is time to start behaving as though you are ready for a different future. While pointing out the flaws and failings of the past leader is a common strategy, you are better than that. Instead of trashing the former leader, speak with enthusiasm about what might be possible with the new person. Avoid mentioning how things have typically been done, the fact that the new leader's bold new idea was actually tried unsuccessfully in the past, or quoting the past leader in any context. Resist expressions of skepticism or suggestions that you miss the former leader. Endeavor to be helpful, demonstrate enthusiasm, look forward, and speak about your excitement for a new era. Doing anything other than this can result in your neck being pierced by the new lion in charge.

RECOGNIZE THE DIFFERENCE BETWEEN AVERSION TO LOSS AND RESISTANCE TO CHANGE

The mood before the meeting was tense, the news was surprising, and the group's reaction was far more negative than positive. As the gathering to announce a significant organizational change came to a close, one of the few people who stood to benefit from the change mused philosophically, "These reactions are all perfectly natural. People are naturally resistant to change."

I found his statement troubling because it assumed that the people doing the objecting were unprogressive, inflexible, and lacking vision. Furthermore, I think the "people don't like change" aphorism is factually incorrect. Many people like change just fine. What they don't like is loss. Or unemployment. Or irrelevance.[1]

Anyone who has ever visited a new restaurant, painted their bedroom a different color, traveled to a never-before-visited city, accepted a promotion, started a new relationship, or found a new favorite song has embraced change. That means the assertion that most people want to keep things exactly the same is ridiculous. We like change as long as it is beneficial to us and the rationale for it makes sense.[2]

That takes me back to the meeting. It felt like many such sessions I had attended before—yet another example of a well-intentioned leader making a rational decision that seemed completely irrational to those most affected by the change. In this case, the leader viewed the situation in the context of national trends and knew that his decision was in line with what similar industries were doing. But here's the thing: most of the people who would be affected by the change had not been following national trends and were completely in the dark about the financial data that influenced the original recommendations. To them, this new organizational design was a solution that had emerged without an obvious problem.

So what lessons can we learn from this situation?

The first is to consult the research on organizational change before embarking on anything that might be considered transformational or even upsetting. Do you lack the time or inclination to do that reading? Here's a recipe for moving ideas forward that builds on several organizational change theories and on the six Ws taught in journalism school: what, why, where, who, when, and how (for which the "w" comes at the end).

Why is this change important? Before announcing a grand plan, expose people to information that makes the need for change obvious. These data sources will depend on your industry or situation and might include consumer choices, patient volume, travel patterns, housing cost trends, or even church attendance rates. Make the need for reform obvious and urgent.

How should the situation be handled? Ask for advice about how to deal with the challenge. You will create a sense of engagement, and you might discover that other people's ideas are better than yours are.

Who will help you? Enlist credible allies who agree that the status quo is no longer viable. Use them to signal that you are not the only one who thinks change is a good idea.

Your allies can help you identify the most vocal skeptics and alert you to the factors that might imperil your plans.

What will it entail? Don't leave room for interpretation and ruminating by keeping details vague. Be crystal clear about what the change will mean so that people can accurately assess how it will affect their status and way of life. Change is not just organizational; it is deeply personal.

Where will it hurt? Be honest about where the pain points will be. Pay cuts? Having to learn something new? More work? Fewer colleagues? Less autonomy? These issues will be apparent soon enough, so you might as well be honest.

When will it happen? Be explicit about deadlines and milestones so that people can track progress and make decisions about when they should leave if they don't want to be a part of the new world order.

Finally, it is worth mentioning a seventh W, the one that appears in the phrase "*what* the hell?" Anticipate anger and name it once it is expressed. Once the change is announced, provide space and time for people to process it and then regroup to respond to questions and concerns.

CREATE THE RIGHT COALITION

When he served as president in the 1950s, Dwight D. Eisenhower was given the moniker the "do-nothing president" because he was not especially visible, charismatic, or obviously involved in high-profile political action. While his critics were not kind to him during his time in the White House, historians eventually recognized that Eisenhower was more strategic and engaged than was originally understood. That's because instead of being out front, Eisenhower tended to use his "hidden hand" to work behind the scenes and allow subordinates to take both credit and political heat.[1]

Eisenhower recognized the power of letting others receive recognition and built quiet coalitions to move his plans forward. If you care more about achieving results than winning applause, his coalition-building approach can work for you as well. But who needs to be part of your coalition? In his book *The Agenda Mover*, Cornell professor Samuel B. Bacharach urges us to classify organizational stakeholders in order to know whom to engage and when, and he offers four categories of people to include.[2]

> **Top dogs.** Bacharach describes *top dogs* as organizational decision makers who have the power to greenlight or torpedo an idea. You may not need their active engagement to move an agenda forward, but you generally need their endorsement.

Gatekeepers. According to Bacharach, *gatekeepers* are under the supervision of the top dogs, but often possess a good deal of authority themselves. They may be other senior leaders or serve a function such as legal counsel for an organization. They will want to weigh in on a proposal before letting it move forward. Knowing that gatekeepers are onboard can be reassuring to other stakeholders.

Gurus. *Gurus* are those who possess expertise or the ability to influence other key decision makers. These might be outside consultants, board members, or friends with specialized experience. Because decision makers look to gurus for guidance and advice, Bacharach argues that their support can be critical.

Players. Bacharach defines *players* as influential stakeholders whose work will be directly impacted by your idea or initiative. Players know how things work and are able to make things happen. If they do not like your idea, they may have the power to block it.

While Bacharach's classification scheme is useful, you may also appreciate the typology advanced by Sara Robinson in her article "6 People You Need to Start a Revolution."[3] While making change or advancing an idea inside an organization is different than launching a social or political revolution, we can make good use of the lessons learned from mass movements such as the civil rights movement, Arab Spring, and the fight for gay marriage, which brought together six types of people:

Activists. Activists are noisemakers and rabble-rousers who create excitement and outrage that can mobilize the masses to demand change. Women's suffragist leader Susan B.

Anthony is an enduring example of an activist who used her intelligence and organizing abilities to incite change.

Intellectuals. It is hard to make a case for change without facts and a coherent roadmap forward. This is where authors, professors, and think-tank members come in. Intellectuals can take anger and outrage and channel them into a rational policy agenda or set of recommendations.

Artists. Professional storytellers, captivating mural painters, songwriters, poets, and filmmakers have the power to create emotion around an issue that moves us to action. Consider photographer Lewis Hine, whose photos of young children working in coal mines and factories in the early part of the twentieth century led the United States to finally adopt restrictions on child labor.[4] Or musician Jay Z, who wrote the song "Spiritual" after Ferguson, Missouri, police shot Michael Brown, an unarmed African American teen, in 2014.[5] The 2019 film *Queen & Slim,* described as "a meditation on a system of justice that treats innocent people as outlaws," was yet another artistic endeavor designed to highlight police violence against African Americans.[6] During the summer of 2020, classical musicians around the world created a moving video in which they played "Albinoni Adagio," a piece that lasted eight minutes and forty-six seconds, the exact duration George Floyd was pinned to the ground by Minneapolis police officers before he suffocated to death.[7] In workplace settings, artists can be tasked with deploying their graphic design expertise, creating campaign slogans, or creating mini-documentaries to outline a problem that needs to be solved.

Insiders. What else is occupying the general counsel's mind at the moment? What's on the next board meeting agenda? What does the chief nursing officer fear most? Insiders know a lot about key decision makers, and we can tap into their knowledge to design a campaign and avoid pitfalls. Insiders can alert us to timing and offer warnings about secret alliances. Insiders may be others with formal power or simply those close to it. Never underestimate the power of an executive assistant.

Supportive elites. Rich and powerful people have the connections, gravitas, and visibility to move ideas from concept to execution, and they can surface in surprising ways. In 2016, *"Gray's Anatomy"* TV star Jesse Williams took the stage to accept the Humanitarian Award at the Black Entertainment Awards. Rather than offering appreciation for the recognition, Williams used his airtime to speak up about police violence against African Americans: "Now, what we've been doing is looking at the data, and we know that police somehow manage to deescalate, disarm, and not kill white people every day. So what's going to happen is we are going to have equal rights and justice in our own country, or we will restructure their function and ours."[8] Inside an organization, supportive elites may be those with position power who are willing to lend their names to a controversial initiative.

The masses. While it is valuable to call on activists, artists, intellectuals, supportive elites, and insiders, we also need the masses to move things forward. So, as you assemble your change coalition, consider how to appeal to average members of your organization so they can speak up for your idea when it is formally introduced.

Building a coalition can be slow and tedious work, but those who are politically shrewd recognize that investing time up front can yield much greater dividends than going it alone. But there is another reason to partner with others. Inside highly political organizations where individuals are constantly vying for power and credit, it can be dangerous to have your name attached to a bold idea, even if it is a good one. It can be smarter to be seen as a member of a broad coalition of supporters. If the idea moves forward, you can claim partial credit, and if it fails, you will not be an obvious target of derision.

REPLACE YOUR ANSWERS WITH QUESTIONS

I once worked with a man who carefully prepared for certain meetings with a "Ten Reasons Why" document. Each time he did this, he fully expected his forceful and well-researched statements move his audience to side with his proposals. He put in a lot of effort, and his points were always salient. To be sure, he delivered his argument with eloquence and passion. He regularly expressed surprise that his strategy rarely worked as he expected. Why was he so often unsuccessful? Because inquiry can be more powerful than ideas and advocacy.[1]

Advocating is stating one's views and may include describing the rationale for a recommendation, expressing judgment, and calling for action. *Inquiry* is a far different approach that involves asking a question, clarifying issues, and sensing points of disagreement. t can be less threatening than advocacy as it invites people to consider new possibilities rather than insisting they do so. In advocacy, we tell others what to think. Through inquiry, we are sometimes able to guide others to accept our perspective. At other times, the inquiry process provides us with information that can lead us to explore an entirely different path or solution. While rhetorical questions and leading questions are sometimes advocacy in disguise,[2] genuine inquiry is a powerful tool for understanding other people's perspectives. Once we understand how others are thinking, we can reevaluate

our own perspectives or use the information we now have to move others closer to our point of view.

Organizational culture expert Edgar Schein suggests that we make a practice of engaging in what he calls "humble inquiry," which he defines as "the fine art of drawing someone out, of asking questions to which you do not already know the answer, of building a relationship based on curiosity and interest in the other person."[3] Why ask rather than tell? Schein asserts that telling is insulting as it implies the other person is not as smart or knowledgeable. Asking, on the other hand, suggests a fair degree of vulnerability as the person asking the question admits there is more to know and learn. Asking also builds trust because the act conveys an interest in the other person.[4]

It is often helpful to begin a conversation by asking others what matters most to them and what outcomes they most want to see. This allows the conversation to move from a rigid position on an issue to a general sense of direction that might be reached in multiple ways. It can be helpful to invite others to describe how they see the situation as a first step and then ask them to give examples of the evidence they are using to reach preliminary conclusions about how to move forward.

Next, invite others to identify information or perspectives you may be missing. Explain, "This is how I see things. What am I failing to consider?" and "What information do you have that I do not?"

If you are trying to move an agenda forward with a group, it can be helpful to start by stating the problem rather than offering your proposed solution. Instead, ask:

"What information do we need to solve this issue?"

"Who needs to be included in this conversation?"

"What data and experience do we already have?"

"What have we tried before, and how did it work?"

"What strategies might we consider?"

If a conversation partner becomes entrenched in their position, ask what is driving the attachment. Do so in a curious, nonconfrontational way that suggests their behavior might be entirely reasonable and that you are simply confused by it.[5]

While inquiry can be effective in cocreating a solution, there are times when a group requires firmer direction. When progress seems stalled, it can be helpful to suggest a solution that others can either agree to or critique.[6] When solutions are cocreated rather than handed down from on high, they are generally more creative, less controversial, and more likely to be embraced by diverse stakeholders. Have a thorny issue to address? Consider asking a question rather than advancing an answer.

STOP SILENCING
THE SKEPTICS

If you are about to launch a major change initiative, it is likely that outside consultants or internal change experts have advised you to plan for potential resistance before announcing your plans. The experts may guide you through the completion of a "change-resistance management plan" to identify and neutralize opponents.[1] These plans have multiple components, key among them anticipating possible questions or concerns in order to prepare responses designed to make clear the dangers of maintaining the status quo. For example:

> A claim of "We can't afford this given our other needs" might be neutralized by replying, "We can't afford not to make strategic investments in our future."

> A potential counterpoint to "This would limit our flexibility" could be "Lack of consistency has created the very problems we are trying to address."

> The assertion "This product seems out of touch with what our customers have asked for" may prompt a response of "It is our job to help our customers realize what they need."

When attempting to move a big idea forward, it is wise to be thoughtful and well prepared, and a change-resistance assessment can identify issues of real or potential concerns

that can be explored with more data or deeper stakeholder conversation. However, the problem with many change-resistance plans is that they are too often used to refute the skeptics, not to hear them. Change initiatives need big ideas, but they also benefit from careful scrutiny and due diligence. People who challenge ideas aren't necessarily opposed to change; they are opposed to making decisions without sufficient evidence or rigorous analysis.

There is a certain irony in attempting to sideline skeptics given that many organizations speak about the importance of hiring innovative people known for thinking deeply. These organizations claim to value people with critical-thinking skills, comfort in challenging assumptions, and the ability to ask hard questions. Then, when these very characteristics are applied in response to news of a change initiative, critical thinkers are accused of blocking progress, nitpicking, and resisting change.

To be sure, some of the people who fight new ideas are protecting their own turf and not truly interested in the good of the larger organization. By listening to the objections, you generally will be able to tell if the critics are naysayers in self-preservation mode or good organizational citizens truly worried about the impact or unintended consequences of your proposed change.

Listening is one of the most important elements of managing a major change. Listen hard enough and you will recognize that most people do not fundamentally resist or dislike change. They resist loss.[2] They resist more work. They resist moving from being considered an expert to appearing incompetent.[3] They resist investing in possibilities that seem uninformed, unethical, or implausible. They especially resist reorganizations or new initiatives designed solely to build a transient leader's personal résumé. Most of all, they resist change when they are excluded from the decision-making process.[4]

I have worked with several consultants who stressed the

importance of identifying skeptics early in the change process so these individuals could be isolated and ultimately silenced. Others cautioned that involving too many actors would just slow things down. It is better, they argued, to build a tight guiding coalition and ignore the naysayers. This is bad advice because skepticism and criticism are essential for innovation.[5] While ignoring or insulting those who are skeptical is not a formula for enduring change in most organizations, it is generally a disastrous strategy in professional settings where smart ideas and informal power tend to trump formal authority. So how can the power of skeptical thinkers be applied in change efforts? Here are three strategies to consider:

Engage skeptics early with questions, not answers. Rather than selling skeptics on solutions, partner with them to clarify the challenges before generating ideas. Once there is agreement on the problems to be solved or opportunities to be explored, debates can focus on how, rather than if, to move forward. While it may seem more pleasant or productive to populate project teams with especially optimistic cheerleaders, harnessing the power and intellect of the chronically frustrated tends to yield better results.[6]

Create structure for dissent and criticism. Invite varied stakeholders to come together to actively dissect and destroy proposals in order to assess their fundamental merits and make them stronger.[7] Ask, "What are all of the reasons this is a bad idea?" "How could we ensure this idea would fail if we were to implement it?" "What could our competition do to put us out of business?" Do not rely solely on subject matter experts to offer criticism. Instead, populate review teams with those who are unfamiliar with the content under consideration. This practice will ensure that fresh perspectives are considered, expose review team members to new ways of thinking, and encourage cross-pollination of both people and ideas.

Create feedback loops. There will come a point when it is time to process varied inputs and make decisions, and not all ideas and suggestions will survive. Rather than rolling out a final product or decision, take time to explain how decisions were made and the factors that led to final results. This will honor those who provided guidance and also increase their ability to make better recommendations the next time they are asked to do so.

When long-term members of an organization express skepticism, they can be criticized as dinosaurs who are stuck in the past, but that is not always fair because they are often the individuals who are worried most about the future. They ask hard questions not because they want to block progress or encourage opposition but because they want to ensure the survival of an organization that is important to them. Often, the skeptics have more history and context than those leading change efforts, so sidelining them is not just disrespectful; it can prove to be quite dangerous. As many ousted or unsuccessful leaders can attest, it is often wiser to embrace one's skeptics than to attempt to silence them.

EXIT WITH GRACE

EXIT BEFORE
THEY CAN FIRE YOU

Receiving an email with the subject line "Career 911" has a way of getting my attention, so when I received this message and saw the author, I assumed one of my former students had been offered yet another new job or promotion and was reaching out for a bit of negotiation advice. I was wrong.

Here is what he shared: "The last time we talked, I was conflicted about my department but excited about the new promotion. Unfortunately, the new job turned out to be a big mistake. My current boss is a micromanager and constantly hovers and criticizes me. I am miserable. He wants to meet with me tomorrow morning before regular office hours, and I have a sinking feeling I'm going to be fired. I am terrified and have no idea how to handle this. Advice???"

My best advice about getting fired is to take preemptive steps to ensure that you leap before the hammer falls. Unfortunately, my former student was too inexperienced to see what a more seasoned person would have recognized as obvious signs that his days were numbered. Because the meeting was just hours away, I offered three pieces of advice.

First, be calm and respectful.[1] Do not raise your voice, argue, or be a jerk. Suck it up and do not say too much. The last thing you want to do is give your boss confirmation that firing you was the right thing to do.

Second, explore options. Because my former student

had been highly successful before his promotion, I suggested he ask if it might be possible to return to that role, at least temporarily.

Third, if termination is the only option, ask for time to make a transition and request a chance to go out on your own terms.

A follow-up call revealed that the early-morning meeting was, as he feared, called to terminate his employment. To his surprise, and mine actually, managing emotions, expressing a desire to redeem himself, and exploring options actually worked, and my former student was given his pre-promotion job back. He will be watched closely and knows that finding a new gig is imperative, but he still has a regular paycheck for at least a while longer.

In an ideal world, leaders would have the courage and good manners to be honest with people who aren't working out, but we do not live in an ideal world. If you sense you are in trouble and are not getting direct feedback about your performance, there are a few signs that it might be time for you to move along. Here are some of them:

You have lots of ideas, but no one likes them. Despite your best efforts to pitch concepts and approaches, none of them ever goes anywhere.

You have plenty of free time. You used to be chronically overcommitted, but your calendar now has plenty of white space. You are not asked to serve on committees or work on key projects, and new work tends to involve tasks that no one else really wants to do.

It takes a long time to get a call returned or an email answered. Is everybody really that busy? No, you are just not a priority.

Vacation and sick time are never a problem. Out sick? No one notices. Want a week off unexpectedly? You are urged to take two.

You are now the director of special projects. While this is not always the case, "special projects" can be code for "work that is not essential."

You have no clue what is going on. You are no longer in the information loop and find yourself blindsided by news everyone else seems to know.[2]

You are a chronic disappointment. Your work is (check one): "inadequate," "not what we agreed upon," or "too late to be useful."

You have less and less autonomy. When you joined your organization, you were expected to be decisive and to make critical choices. Now you have to request permission for almost everything.

Communication is increasingly formal. While you used to engage in quick hallway conversations about new initiatives or special requests, you now communicate via formal messages that begin with "As we discussed on [insert date]."

If this list describes what you are experiencing in your current role, don't invest energy in trying to turn things around. Instead, take the hints and start looking for your next opportunity. It is almost always better to quit than to be fired.

BE PREPARED
TO WALK AWAY

Have you ever observed another person's career train wreck? Have you looked on in horror, and what seems like slow motion, as otherwise smart people demonstrate profound naïveté about how to navigate their careers? I can think of three especially disastrous career crashes. As I watched each unfold, I found myself wanting to shout, "No, no. Don't do it!" Unfortunately, in each case, I arrived too late to be helpful. I was able to diagnose what had caused the derailment, but I did not arrive on the scene in time to prevent the damage from being done.

Case one was a situation in which a very talented person was encouraged to apply for a job she didn't want in order to use it as leverage to increase her salary. When she succeeded in getting an offer, she met with her boss to share the news and said, basically, "I've received this great new offer. What will you offer to keep me?" The response in this case was "It would be wrong to hold you back; best of luck to you." She ended up staying but found herself without the trust or political capital she had enjoyed before the attempt to increase her salary with an outside offer.

Case two involved a candidate who, after receiving an offer for her dream job, was coached to express disdain for a salary offer and encouraged to counter by reimagining the job and asserting that the bigger role was worth a 30 percent higher salary. The response was worse than "I'm sorry; that's not possible." Instead, it was "Thank you but never mind."

Case three involved a man who had received a hint of interest from a prospective employer and was encouraged by a good friend to use that potential opportunity to secure a promotion. He scripted his ask with care: "I really enjoy working here, but the idea of a leadership role is, of course, hard to turn down. If you could match the opportunity, I would consider staying." It was a double blow when his current employer failed to offer anything new, and the prospective employer did not come through either.

A key strategy in good negotiation is to have a backup plan and some wiggle room. Asking questions about what might be possible is wiser than issuing ultimatums that may eventually be shot down. If you aren't prepared to walk away from your current situation, it's not smart to play hardball.

For those who think using an outside offer is a good way to leverage a promotion or pay increase in your current organization, you should know there is a growing body of research that indicates that retention offers aren't good for employers.[1] While a boost in pay may temporarily elevate employee satisfaction, research has found that once employees have explored other organizations, they tend to psychically "break up" with their current employer and demonstrate less engagement. As a result, employers are then paying more to receive less. Retention offers for employees are not generally good for the employee either. The factors that initially led them to pursue new possibilities rarely resolve themselves, and so they end up getting paid a bit more but still have to do work or engage with people they don't really like.

If you are a candidate with a job offer, being honest about your hopes and aspirations and the issues you are weighing in considering the offer is the best way to demonstrate integrity in the negotiation process. Honesty is generally effective for current employees as well. Having regular conversations about what you enjoy, where you see yourself contributing, and your hopes for the future can be the best way to get on the radar for new opportunities and ascertain what might be possible. These conversations may reveal that you are highly valued and under consideration for opportunities you had not even considered. They may also reveal that you are not viewed as critical to your organization's success. Either way, it will give you the information you need to chart a path forward.

Whether you are a candidate or a current employee, it is important to determine what it will take for you to stay or to go. Once you are clear about this, it is easier to ask for what you want and to spell out your next steps if it is not possible to honor your request. It is essential, however, to understand that asking does not always lead to getting, and your personal credibility will be destroyed if you threaten to go and then stick around instead.

CUT YOUR LOSSES QUICKLY

A friend of mine spent several weeks gushing about a new job she was going to begin after wrapping up a few years as a private consultant. She was ecstatic about landing a strategic role free of the annoying day-to-day operational issues and money pressures she had dealt with by running her own business. "Best of all," she exclaimed, "I will get paid to think!" All did not go as she planned, however.

Week one had her sounding tentative. In week two, she started sounding nervous. By week three, she looked drained as she laid out her situation to a group of us who met after work for what turned out to be a sad hour rather than the happy hour we had planned. She was miserable.

Instead of working for someone recognized as innovative, there was a last-minute and allegedly "just temporary" switch to someone else, who clearly didn't like her. Instead of doing strategic work, she was assigned detailed-oriented projects. Despite being promised autonomy, her schedule was tightly managed and monitored. The work was tedious, and the conditions were oppressive. Worst of all, she learned the "temporary" manager was going to be permanent.

When my friend asked members of her brain trust what to do next and noted that she felt fortunate to have enough money in the bank to weather a few months of unemployment, feedback was mixed. About half of the group suggested she cut her losses immediately and resign. I was in the camp that suggested patience and asked, "Who can make a reasonable assessment about a new job after just three weeks?"

I have to admit that I am a pretty cautious person because it's hard to buy groceries with a fistful of principles, but my advice to her in this case was based on more than economics. Quitting a job after three weeks when working retail or delivering pizzas is one thing, but quitting a decent-level professional position before less than a month had passed struck me as petulant and irresponsible. "Make yourself valuable while expressing confusion about your situation," I suggested. "Making a statement by storming out isn't going to get you anything and isn't really fair to the people who chose you over everyone else."

My friend went back to work and tried what I suggested. While the job did not work out in the end, she managed to salvage the time in a creative way. She prepared a report that detailed recommendations for improving the organizational structure as well as a list of potential process improvements. She then provided these to the CEO who originally hired her in exchange for a reference that referred to her as a short-term consultant rather than a failed employee. Both individuals saved face in the end.

At some point in your career, you may face a similar "this is not what I expected" situation and discover that your new dream job is more like a nightmare. At first, you might second-guess your initial gut instincts and say to yourself, "I'm new, and I am just figuring things out. This is just all part of the transition process. My colleagues will warm to me soon. The person I report to is just under stress. I came at a tough time, but it will be better soon."

Over time, you will come to understand that it's not you; it's them. That's when the hard decision has to be made: Do you stick it out, or do you plan an immediate exit strategy? It is normal to be concerned about looking like a job-hopper or even a failure, but tolerating misery can deplete the energy we need to find something better.

There is no easy answer to the "How long is long enough?" question, but once you've decided to move along, there are ways to manage the messaging about why you left or plan to leave early.

Complete honesty might not be the best policy here. While you do not want to lie, it's best not to go on and on about nasty coworkers, soul-crushing work, or a boss with no integrity. All that would make potential employers wonder what you might say about them one day. Instead, consider expressing disappointment. "After about a month, it became clear that the job was not what I believed it to be. I don't have a history of leaving positions quickly, so I had to think hard about this and what it might mean for my career. During the brief time I've been there, I have accomplished several things I am proud of, including [insert your accomplishments here]." If you have no accomplishments, you might consider noting the things you have learned.

If possible, spend concentrated time establishing connections with people who will speak well of you and back up your story when you are ready to make your move: "He has developed some exceptional marketing materials during his short time here, and we are going to miss that if he leaves." Or, perhaps, "She's masterful at process mapping and positioned us to streamline our approach to patient intake."

Consider who might be willing to tell your transition story better and more convincingly than you. One person might reveal, "I think the creative director changed her mind about what she needed for the role," while another might state, "The job description that was posted was inaccurate. I think Ignacio expected to have a good deal more autonomy."

If you had a reasonable track record before the nightmare job, a one-time blip is not likely to make you a pariah. If you have little work experience or your work history is spotty, you might want to suck it up for at least a year and do everything possible to build a list of accomplishments. Then, as soon as the twelve-month mark rolls around, have your résumé ready, a portfolio of accomplishments well documented, and a list of internal and external colleagues who will speak well of you in a conversation with your next employer.

It is disappointing to find yourself in a role or organization that is not what you imagined or even what you were promised. While it is true that many of us struggle to acclimate in new environments, we need to honor our inner voice when it tells us we have made a terrible mistake.

ALWAYS LEAVE WELL

The time has come, and you are ready to go. You have accepted a new job with people who seem to think you're amazing, and you are eager to make a fresh start. First, however, you have to share the big news with people in your current organization, and that prospect has you feeling a little nervous.

You have a lot to say, and you're wondering how to say it. You feel annoyed that people assumed you would be around forever and never offered you the attention they gave to more obvious flight risks. You offered to take on more responsibilities to ward off professional boredom, but you could never garner their support for giving you a larger or more diverse portfolio. Most troubling, your bosses consistently rewarded the self-promoters while ignoring solid citizens like you who quietly delivered results without a lot of fanfare.

With a job offer in hand, this feels like a good time to detail the years of disappointment that finally prompted you to consider a new opportunity. But is it? As you write your letter of resignation and think about what you plan to say regarding your pending departure, should you be completely honest or should you bury your bitterness in an effort to be professional and polite?

Here's a tip: Take your laptop or a pad of paper and write the resignation letter that you would love to send. Outline the various injustices you endured and make a detailed list of improvements that should be implemented to ensure that

you are the last person to feel mistreated. Be as detailed as possible when describing the slights you experienced and how they made you feel. Mention the first time that you thought about leaving and explain why you regret delaying your departure. Also, prepare a second response—briefer but similarly themed—that you can offer verbally or in writing when people express surprise about your departure.

Review both drafts, correct punctuation and grammar, and then set them aside to read the next day. When tomorrow comes, read them again and make additional edits. The next step? Destroy both documents.

Having deleted your well-crafted messages, begin to prepare something vague and professionally appropriate that you can actually deliver or say in public.

The neutral zone between your old life and your new one can be a treacherous space. When you have a firm offer to move on, you may feel emboldened to speak truth to power and ensure that those who let you down know that actions have consequences. You may also be tempted to punish your former colleagues, perhaps leaving loose ends that will make life especially hard for them after you are gone. Leaving well is a far better option, and here are some tips for how to go out on a high note.

Before you deliver any news to anyone, make sure your affairs are in order. Make copies of anything you might need, to the degree that is allowable. Make sure you no longer need your soon-to-be-old work email address and anything connected to it. Remove anything from your workspace that would cause discomfort or embarrassment were it to be discovered by others. One of my new employees once found a folded piece of paper that read "I am independently wealthy and bring in one million dollars in passive income annually" stuck in the back of a desk drawer of the former cubicle resident. Every time the former desk occupant comes to mind, we all think about his hokey wealth affirmation statement. Be thorough as you empty your workspace.

Next, offer your resignation in person. At the end of the conversation, provide a letter of resignation in writing. Give as much notice as possible, but be open to the possibility that you may be asked to leave sooner than you expected. Be sure that you have taken home anything you might need from your workspace before delivering the news.

When asked why you are leaving, speak of what drew you to the new opportunity rather than what prompted you to start looking in the first place.

Finish strong. Wrap up projects, complete assignments, and honor your commitments. If you slack off toward the end, that is how you will be remembered.

Send thank-you notes to everyone who supported you so they will think well of you after you have gone.

Leave your affairs in good order. Provide a detailed project list. Make sure your files are accessible and well organized; create a roadmap so that your content can be accessed later. Delete or throw away content that you probably should have tossed or deleted years ago and leave your workspace clean and tidy.

Offer to be a resource as questions arise in the future and honor your word when a former colleague calls you.

While it may be tempting to leave overly ripe fruit or a juicy roast beef sandwich with extra mayonnaise in a desk drawer for others to find weeks after you have gone, resist the urge.

Once you are gone, be gone. Do not check in. Do not try to stay up to date on internal workings. Do not offer advice. Do not comment on your successor's performance. Yes, you have important insights to share, but the time for sharing is now over.

In your excitement—or relief—about leaving, it may not occur to you that you might want to return one day. By leaving responsibly and quietly, a return invitation might actually be possible should you want it down the road.

CONCLUSION

DO YOUR PART TO REDUCE ORGANIZATIONAL POLITICS

Imagine being part of an organization where the vision and key priorities are obvious, uniformly known, and well understood. Think about what it would be like to be part of an enterprise where decisions are made based on evidence and objective criteria rather than paying back favors or relying on gut instincts. How about an organization that distributes rewards and recognition based on who does the best work and collaborates most effectively? Picture what it would be like to work in an organization where words have no secret meanings, colleagues are invested in each other's success, the process for requesting and acquiring resources is straightforward, and the indicators of success are clearly documented. Does this sound like a place where you would like to be?

Organizations characterized by candor, fairness, and even kindness do not require special technology platforms, complex systems, or long and complicated procedure manuals. It is, frankly, not that hard to create the kind of workplace in which most of us would thrive. Given this and the fact that those who work in highly political environments report they are stressed, unhappy, cynical, unproductive, and eager to leave,[1] there is clearly a business case for attempting to eliminate negative political behavior. So why don't organizational leaders do more to reduce negative and sometimes debilitating organizational politics?

Is it possible that they benefit from keeping people in the dark and manipulating decision-making? Do they engage in ruthless organizational politics because they enjoy wielding power and creating fear? If that is the case, they are not worthy to be leaders. If, by chance, unhealthy political behavior exists because no one seems to know how to stop it, here are a few ideas to create a healthier and more productive workplace.

Publish and regularly review organizational values

A key first step toward a less political and more inspiring organizational culture is being explicit about values. Clearly stated values tell us what matters most, how we should behave, and the kinds of people who are most likely to be successful. If you visit a hospital, a car rental agency, or even an insurance company, you might see a list of values framed and hanging on the wall. Should you see them, be sure to ask the people you interact with how those values came to be established and whether they are real or just wall art. Importantly, ask if they had a hand in shaping them. Effective organizational values are created through meaningful conversations with people at all levels of an organization. If they are artfully created in an executive suite, they may well be designed to serve a public relations purpose rather than to offer members of the organization a compass for navigating and evaluating their behavior.

Cocreate unit-level working agreements

As discussed earlier in this book, working agreements, sometimes called "ground rules" or "group agreements," offer guidance about how members should interact, how decisions will be made, and the consequences for failing to abide by group standards. Working agreements are only effective when they are created by the group that is intended to live by them, so when new members join a group, it is wise to revisit the agreements to ensure they reflect the commitments of the evolving team, unit, or department.

Hire the right people

Hiring new colleagues is one of the most important things we can do to shape the future of an organization. The organizations that care most about their cultures are thoughtful and methodical about selecting new people. They ask candidates probing questions about their work styles, collaboration preferences, openness to feedback, adaptability, sources of motivation, and competitive nature. They also seek to understand what makes them angry, their history of sacrificing personal interests for the common good, how they would respond to unethical behavior, and whether they prefer to see themselves as individuals or members of a group. If a candidate appears demanding or arrogant in the interview process, you can be sure that behavior will be magnified once they are safely employed, and everyone else will suffer as a result.

Don't permit workarounds

In highly political organizations, certain actors feel it is their right to ignore protocols in order to get what they want or need. This is especially true when policies, procedures, and protocols are overly cumbersome or complicated for no apparent reason. Busy and important people don't have time for administrivia, right? In organizations with low levels of organizational politics, it is generally easier to get things done. Processes are outlined and often automated, and working around the rules can be harder than actually following them. Importantly, organizations with low levels of organizational politics do not permit workarounds, and those who attempt to work around systems both fail to get what they want and also come to understand that there are consequences for failing to follow the rules.

Be transparent about success indicators

Few things are more frustrating than working hard only to discover that one's efforts are not valued or appreciated. In highly political organizations, the rules and success indicators are often unclear and ever changing. In less political organizations, success standards are clearly described, results are easy to measure, and members know what is required to meet or exceed performance standards.

Make pay decisions transparent

Few organizational practices are more political than compensation protocols. While pay practices and decisions are considered confidential in many organizations, there is a national movement to make pay practices more transparent. Providing employees with access to their colleagues' salaries makes it more difficult to discriminate for illegal reasons, to demonstrate favoritism, or to use pay as a strategy for building supporters and allies. That said, simply providing salary data is insufficient to make pay decisions make sense.

Strategic organizations make sure their employees understand how pay rates are calculated. For example, pay may be based on data available from comparable organizations, and the organization can share the source of salary surveys used to determine pay ranges for various titles. Pay may also be determined based on where the organization wants to position itself among competitors. For example, a missile defense organization may seek to be the pay leader in any community in which it exists as a strategy for attracting and retaining the top engineers in a given region. Pay based on labor market scarcity is a common strategy. When the demand for data scientists exceeds supply, individuals in these roles can command higher salaries than those with comparable levels of education and experience in related fields. If this is the case in your organization, be open about it. The criticality of roles is another strategy that can be employed to establish pay. For example, if creating an exceptional customer experience is a hotel's signature, it may pay valet drivers and registration desk employees much more than they can earn in a competitor's hotel. This is reasonable as long as everyone else in the organization understands the strategy.

Regardless of how pay decisions are made, being transparent about the methodology employed and the path required to receive a pay increase will create a sense of trust among employees and signal to supervisors that they are expected to pay their employees in accordance with established guidelines.

Practice compassionate candor

It might surprise you to learn that offering regular feedback is a strategy for reducing perceptions of negative organizational politics,[2] but if you think about it, this makes sense. When employees receive regular information on how they are doing, it is easier for them to make sense of how pay and promotion decisions are being made and even why certain people are offered challenging and high-profile assignments.

There is an art to providing useful feedback, and not everyone is brave enough to provide it. In her book *Radical Candor: How to Get What You Want by Saying What You Mean*, Kim Scott argues that we too often withhold vital performance information from our employees because we do not want to hurt their feelings.[3] Scott claims that our efforts to be kind are actually quite cruel because we are withholding the information and guidance our employees need to be successful. She calls this misguided kindness "ruinous empathy" and contrasts it with her preferred approach of "radical candor," the practice of offering regular and direct feedback motivated by genuine care about the other person's success.

Offer opportunities for voice

Looking to improve a system or enhance customer satisfaction? Before you call in the consultants, start by talking to employees on the front lines. They generally know what works and what doesn't, what frustrates clients, and which components of their work requirements add no value. A structured process for regularly engaging with employees at all levels of an organization is a smart and inexpensive way to gather intelligence.[4] And it's not enough to take their advice; when employees offer smart ideas for improvement, they should be recognized for their efforts to make things better.

Open the books

When I encourage organizational leaders to share information about costs and revenues with employees at all levels of their organization, I am usually met with great skepticism. Many of these leaders tell me employees will not be interested, and they express doubt that many of them would even be capable of understanding the numbers. When I respond that being more transparent about their financial situation can improve trust and reduce perceptions of organizational politics,[5] they seem curious about how this could be possible.

It will not surprise you to know that when employees understand the numbers and how their behaviors and daily decisions can influence profitability or at least sustainability, they are better positioned to understand how their daily decisions can contribute to the bottom line and to articulate and accept the rationale for decisions and recommendations. Again, having information reduces the sense that decisions are being made based on factors other than sound evidence.

Feeling that their organizations are overly political is discouraging to employees because it suggests that succeeding or even surviving requires discovering the unwritten rules, forging alliances with the right people, and being careful not to upset or alienate the wrong people. Being on constant alert for danger does little to encourage innovation or creativity[6]—attributes critical for organizations to survive in the long term. Creating a sense of psychological safety, being explicit about expectations, sharing information, and refusing to reward rule breakers are just some of the strategies organizational leaders can employ to create workplaces that encourage everyone to be successful.

EVIL OR STRATEGIC?
SOME FINAL THOUGHTS

Most of us would like to think of our organizations as orderly, rational places where decisions are made with solid data and sophisticated analysis. It can be a disappointment when we learn that corporations, small businesses, nonprofit agencies, schools, universities, social clubs, religious organizations, and even homeowners associations tend to reject logic and are often driven by personalities, invisible coalitions, and the self-interest of those who have personal agendas and a need for power and control. We can get mad about this, or we can acknowledge that political dynamics exist and attempt to navigate them in a fashion that is aligned with our personal values.

We began this book asserting that we can navigate organizational politics ethically and honorably and that we need to shake off the commonly held perception that actively engaging in organizational politics makes us mean or manipulative. The key is to distinguish political activities designed to elevate ideas or advance our agendas using ethical principles from those activities designed to advance interests by damaging or demoralizing others.

Differentiating between these two approaches should not be too hard, so let's close by reflecting on advice included in this book to evaluate whether some common organizational politics plays are evil or simply strategic. Ready? Here goes:

Example 1
- Building upon a good idea and offering credit to the person who inspired you? *Strategic.*
- Stealing someone else's idea? *Evil.*

239

Example 2

- Challenging flawed logic by asking clarifying questions? *Strategic.*
- Intentionally humiliating a colleague in front of others? *Evil.*

Example 3

- Calling a meeting to understand all of the factors that led to a bad decision? *Strategic.*
- Shifting blame to someone who was only tangentially involved? *Evil.*

Example 4

- Explaining that you are not in a position to reveal all the facts? *Possibly strategic.*
- Creating confusion to make others feel unstable? *Evil.*

Example 5

- Customizing a message based on a decision maker's thinking style? *Strategic.*
- Lying to influence a key decision maker? *Evil.*

Example 6

- Withholding information from those who will abuse it? *Possibly strategic.*
- Spreading misinformation to damage someone's reputation? *Definitely evil.*

Example 7

- Asking a colleague to nominate you for a high-profile project team? *Strategic.*
- Casting doubts about the integrity of a colleague going for a role you want? *Evil.*

You have read this book because you want to get things done, advance professionally, or simply improve your ability to understand or work with people who are secretive, calculating, or just hard to read. As much as you want to be more effective in navigating organizational politics, I bet you also want to be considered a good person while doing so. The good news is that you can be both successful and highly ethical. I hope *The Organizational Politics Playbook* has offered you some useful strategies to make sense of political moves, anticipate and counter dirty tricks, and, importantly, achieve what you want in a way that is ethical and honorable.

ENDNOTES

Preface: "I Don't Do Politics" Is Not an Option

1 Petty, A. (June 20, 2011). Leadership Caffeine: 4 Ideas for Navigating Organizational Politics. https://artpetty.com/2011/06/20/leadership-caffeine-4-ideas-for-navigating-organizational-politics/.

2 Pfeffer, J. (2010). *Power: Why Some People Have It and Others Don't*. New York: HarperBusiness;.

3 Machiavelli, N. (1984). *The Prince* (1513). New York: Bantam.

4 Greene, R., Elffers, J. (2015). *The 48 Laws of Power*. London: Profile Books.

5 Lynskey, D. (December 3, 2012). Robert Greene on His 48 Laws of Power: "I'm Not Evil—I'm a Realist." *The Guardian*. https://www.theguardian.com/books/2012/dec/03/robert-greene-48-laws-of-power.

Playbook Move 1: Know What It Means to Be "Political"

1 Landells, E. M., Albrech, S. L. (2017). The Positives and Negatives of Organizational Politics: A Qualitative Study. *Journal of Business and Psychology*. 32(1):41–58. https://doi.org/10.1007/s10869-015-9434-5.

2 Chang, C. H., Rosen, C. C., Levy, P. E. (2009). The Relationship between Perceptions of Organizational Politics and Employee Attitudes, Strain, and Behavior: A Meta-Analytic Examination. *Academy of Management Journal*. 52(4):779–801. https://doi.org/10.5465/amj.2009.43670894.

3 Djurdjevic, E., Rosen, C. C., Conroy, S. A., Rawski, S. L., Sosna, K. U. (2019). The Influence of Political Climate on Job Pursuit Intentions and the Moderating Effect of Machiavellianism. *International Journal of Selection and Assessment*. 27(2):180–192. https://doi.org/10.1111/ijsa.12242.

4 Aristotle. (1995). *Politics*. Oxford: Oxford University Press.

5 Lasswell, H. (1936). *Who Gets What, When, and How*. New York: Whittlesey House.

6   Brandon, R., Seldman, M. (2004). *Survival of the Savvy*. New York: Free Press, 2.

7   Ferris, G. R., Perrewé, P. L., Daniels, S. R., Lawong, D., Holmes, J. J. (2017). Social Influence and Politics in Organizational Research: What We Know and What We Need to Know. *Journal of Leadership & Organizational Studies*. 24(1):5–19. https://doi.org/10.1177/1548051816656003.

8   Kotter, J. (1985). *Power and Influence*. New York: Free Press.

9   Ferris, G. R. (2007). Treadway, D. C., Perrewé, P. L., Brouer, R. L., Douglas, C., Lux, S. (2007). Political Skill in Organizations. *Journal of Management*. 33(3):290–320. https://doi.org/10.1177/0149206307300813.

10 Leslie, J., & Gentry, W. (2013, June 19). Why You Have To Be A Politician At Your Job . Forbes. https://www.forbes.com/2010/05/25/office-politics-psychology-leadership-managing-ccl.html?sh=5eef3c605b15.

11 Goffman, E. (1959). *The Presentation of Self in Everyday Life*. New York: Doubleday.

12 Ferris. (2007).

13 Ferris. (2007).

14 Salovey, P., Mayer, J. D. (1990). Emotional Intelligence. *Imagination, Cognition and Personality*. 9(3):185–211. https://doi.org/10.2190/DUGG-P24E-52WK-6CDG.

15 Ferris, G. R., Perrewe, P. L., Douglas, C. (2002). Social Effectiveness in Organizations: Construct Validity and Research Directions. *Journal of Leadership & Organizational Studies*. 9(1):49–63. https://doi-org.ezproxy3.library.arizona.edu/10.1177/107179190200900104.

16 Ferris et al. (2007).

Playbook Move 2: Determine Who Has Power and Why

1   Weber, M. (1958). The Three Types of Legitimate Rule. *Berkeley Publications in Society and Institutions*. 4(1):1–11. Translated by Hans Gerth.

2   Keltner, D. (2016). *The Power Paradox: How We Gain and Lose Influence*. New York: Penguin.

3 Raven, B. H. (1965). Social Influence and Power. In: Steiner ID, Fishbein M, eds. *Current Studies in Social Psychology*). New York: Holt, Rinehart, Winston. 371–382.

4 Grant, A. M. (2013). *Give and Take: A Revolutionary Approach to Success.* New York: Penguin Random House.

Playbook Move 3: Learn the Dirty Tricks

1 DuBrin, A. J. (1990). *Winning Office Politics: DuBrin's Guide for the 90s.* Paramus, NJ: Prentice Hall Press.

2 Kacmar, K. M., Baron, R. A. (1999). Organizational Politics: The State of the Field, Links to Related Processes, and an Agenda for Future Research. *Research in Personnel and Human Resources Management.* 17:1–39.

3 Peyton, P. R. (2004). *Dignity at Work: Eliminate Bullying and Create a Positive Working Environment.* New York: Brunner-Routledge.

4 Bruckmüller, S., Branscombe, N. R. (2010). The Glass Cliff: When and Why Women Are Selected as Leaders in Crisis Contexts. *British Journal of Social Psychology.* 49(3):433–451. https://doi.org/10.1348/014466609X466594.

5 Kacmar & Baron. (1999).

6 Strategic Services. (January 17, 1944). Simple Sabotage Field Manual. Declassified per guidance from the Chief/DRRB CIA Declassification Center. https://www.cia.gov/news-information/featured-story-archive/2012-featured-story-archive/CleanedUOSSSimpleSabotage_sm.pdf.

7 Machiavelli, N. (1984). *The Prince* (1513). New York: Bantam.

8 Strategic Services. (1944). 29.

9 Strategic Services. (1944). 1.

10 Strategic Services. (1944). 28.

Playbook Move 4: Separate the Powerful from the Posers

1 Cooper, S. (2016). *100 Tricks to Appear Smart in Meetings: How to Get By without Even Trying.* Kansas City, MI: Andrews McMeel Publishing, A Division of Andrews McMeel Universal.

2 Ryken, L., Wilhoit, J., Longman, T., Duriez, C., Penney, D., Reid, D. G. (1998). Right, Right Hand. *Dictionary of Biblical Imagery*. Downers Grove, IL: Intervarsity Press. 727–728.

Playbook Move 5: Embrace Impression Management

1 Kingo, A., West-Rosenthal, L., Santos, M., Fish, Q., Tansey, C. (May 13, 2020). How C-Suite Women of Color Have Powerfully Redefined Executive Presence. https://www.workingmother.com/new-executive-presence.

2 Hewlett. (2014).

3 Guarino, J. (January 8, 2020). Vocal Fry Is Everyone's Issue. https://www.instituteofpublicspeaking.com/vocal-fry-is-everyones-issue/.

4 King, M. L., Jr. (August 16, 1967). Where Do We Go from Here? Speech presented at 11th Annual SCLC Convention. Atlanta, GA.

5 Cuddy, A. J., Fiske, S. T., Glick, P. (2008). Warmth and Competence as Universal Dimensions of Social Perception: The Stereotype Content Model and the BIAS Map. *Advances in Experimental Social Psychology*. 40:61–149.

6 Neffinger, J., Kohut, M. (2013). *Compelling People: The Hidden Qualities That Make Us Influential*. New York: Hudson Street Press. 17.

7 Cuddy, A. J., Glick, P., Beninger, A. (2011). The Dynamics of Warmth and Competence Judgments, and Their Outcomes in Organizations. *Research in Organizational Behavior*. 31:73–98. https://doi.org/10.1016/j.riob.2011.10.004.

8 Surakka, V., Hietanen, J. K. (1998). Facial and Emotional Reactions to Duchenne and Non-Duchenne Smiles. *International Journal of Psychophysiology*. 29(1):23–33. https://doi.org/10.1016/S0167-8760(97)00088-3.

9 Carli, L. L., LaFleur, S. J., Loeber, C. C. (1995). Nonverbal Behavior, Gender, and Influence. *Journal of Personality and Social Psychology*. 68(6):1030. https://doi.org/10.1037/0022-3514.68.6.1030. Also Mehrabian, A., Ferris, S. R. (1967). Inference of Attitudes from Nonverbal Communication in Two Channels. *Journal of Consulting Psychology*. 31(3):248. https://doi.org/10.1037/h0024648.

10 Talley, L., Temple, S. (2015). How Leaders Influence Followers through the Use of Nonverbal Communication. *Leadership & Organization Development Journal.* 36(1):69–80. https://doi.org/10.1108/LODJ-07-2013-0107.

11 Neffinger. (2013).

12 Schwarz, C. (April 8, 2015). Julia Louis-Dreyfus Hates the "Clinton Thumb." *The Washington Post.* http://wapo.st/1CgyIG4?tid=ss_tw.

13 Neffinger, J., Kohut, M. (October 23, 2012). Compelling People. [Video File]. https://www.youtube.com/watch?v=HORh6L7gUVg.

Playbook Move 6: Consider Being Likable

1 Huang, K., Yeomans, M., Brooks, A.W, Minson, J., Gino, F. (2017). It Doesn't Hurt to Ask: Question-Asking Increases Liking. *Journal of Personality and Social Psychology.* 113(3):430. https://doi.org/10.1037/pspi0000097.

2 Covey, S. R. (2004). *The 7 Habits of Highly Effective People: Powerful Lessons in Personal Change.* New York: Simon and Schuster.

3 Casciaro, T., Lobo, M. S. (2005). Competent Jerks, Lovable Fools, and the Formation of Social Networks. *Harvard Business Review.* 83(6):92–99.

Playbook Move 7: Use the Power of Scarcity

1 Ghodsee, K. (May 26, 2016). Say Nothing or Say No? *Chronicle of Higher Education.* https://chroniclevitae.com/news/1412-say-nothing-or-say-no.

2 Anari, D. S. (August 13, 2019). The Law of Specialization in Personal Branding. *Forbes.* https://www.forbes.com/sites/forbescoachescouncil/2019/08/13/the-law-of-specialization-in-personal-branding/.

3 Lynn, M. (1992). The Psychology of Unavailability: Explaining Scarcity and Cost Effects on Value. *Basic and Applied Social Psychology.* 13(1):3–7.

Playbook Move 8: Say "No" Graciously

1 Goleman, D., Boyatzis, R. E., McKee, A. (2002). *The New Leaders.* London: Little Brown.

2 Church, A. H. (1997). Managerial Self-Awareness in High-Performing Individuals in Organizations. *Journal of Applied Psychology*. 82:281–292. https://doi.org/10.1037/0021-9010.82.2.281.

3 Rahim, H. (March 16, 2017). Why Self-Aware Leaders Are More Productive and Effective. *The Telegraph*. https://www.telegraph.co.uk/connect/better-business/leadership/self-aware-leaders-more-productive-and-effective/.

4 Dierdorff, E. C., Rubin, R. S. (2015). We're Not Very Self-Aware, Especially at Work. *Harvard Business Review*. https://hbr.org/2015/03/research-were-not-very-self-aware-especially-at-work.

5 Eurich, T. (2018). *Insight: The Surprising Truth about How Others See Us, How We See Ourselves, and Why the Answers Matter More Than We Think*. New York: Currency.

Playbook Move 12: Avoid Shining Too Brightly

1 Feather, N. T. (1989). Attitudes towards the High Achiever: The Fall of the Tall Poppy. *Australian Journal of Psychology*. 41(3):239–267. https://doi.org/10.1080/00049538908260088.

2 Kim, E., Glomb, T. M. (2010). Get Smarty Pants: Cognitive Ability, Personality, and Victimization. *Journal of Applied Psychology*. 95(5):889. https://doi.org/10.1037/a0019985.

3 Feather, N. T. (2012). Tall Poppies, Deservingness and Schadenfreude. *The Psychologist*. June 25:434–437. https://thepsychologist.bps.org.uk/volume-25/edition-6/tall-poppies-deservingness-and-schadenfreude.

4 Kim, E., Glomb, T. M. (2014). Victimization of High Performers: The Roles of Envy and Work Group Identification. *Journal of Applied Psychology*. 99(4):619. https://doi.org/10.1037/a0035789.

Playbook Move 13: Strive to Be Noticed

1 Grant, A. (March 20, 2018). Adam Grant Can Help You Coax Generosity out of Your Grumpiest Coworker. *Fast Company*. https://www.fastcompany.com/40545869/adam-grant-can-help-you-coax-generosity-out-of-your-grumpiest-coworker.

Playbook Move 14: Practice Party Tricks for Introverts

1 Cain, S. (2013). *Quiet: The Power of Introverts in a World That Can't Stop Talking.* London: Viking.

2 Stillman, J. (June 23, 2016). If You're an Introvert, Here's How to Survive Your Next Work Party. *Inc.* https://www.inc.com/jessica-stillman/if-you-re-an-introvert-here-s-how-to-survive-your-next-work-party.html.

3 Dembling, S. (November 20, 2009). Party Survival Tactics for Introverts. https://www.psychologytoday.com/us/blog/the-introverts-corner/200911/party-survival-tactics-introverts.

4 Thorpe, J. R. (July 28, 2016). 7 Essential Party Tips for Introverts. https://www.bustle.com/articles/175155-7-essential-party-tips-for-introverts.

5 Stillman, J. (2016).

6 Clark, D. (August 15, 2014). Networking for Introverts. *Harvard Business Review.* https://hbr.org/2014/08/networking-for-introverts.

Playbook Move 15: Build Yourself a Brain Trust

1 Tugwell, R. G. (1968). *The Brains Trust.* New York: Viking Press.

Playbook Move 16: Keep Your Ambition in Check

1 Dawsey, J. (November 17, 2016). Regrets? Chris Christie Has a Few. *Politico.* https://www.politico.com/magazine/story/2017/11/17/chris-christie-regrets-profile-2017-215832.

2 Steinberg, A. (December 27, 2017). Does Chris Christie Still Have White House Aspirations? *Insider New Jersey.* https://www.insidernj.com/chris-christie-still-white-house-aspirations/.

Playbook Move 20: Get Your Name in the Chalice

1 United States Conference on Catholic Bishops. (February 21, 2013). How Is a New Pope Chosen? http://www.usccb.org/about/leadership/holy-see/francis/how-is-a-new-pope-chosen.cfm and BBC News. Also, Conclave: How Cardinals Elect a Pope. https://www.bbc.com/news/world-21412589.

2 Grant, A. M. (2013). *Give and Take: A Revolutionary Approach to Success.* New York: Penguin.

Playbook Move 21: Behave Well When You're Not the One

1   Nawaz, S. (October 31, 2017). Get the Actionable Feedback You Need to Get Promoted. https://hbr.org/2017/10/get-the-actionable-feedback-you-need-to-get-promoted.

Playbook Move 23: Don't Let Mean People Destroy Your Career

1   Arkes, H. R., Blumer, C. (1985). The Psychology of Sunk Cost. *Organizational Behavior and Human Decision Processes*. 35(1):124–140. https://doi.org/10.1016/0749-5978(85)90049-4.

2   Cohen, J. A., Berliner, L., Mannarino, A. (2010). Trauma Focused CBT for Children with Co-occurring Trauma and Behavior Problems. *Child Abuse & Neglect*. 34(4):215–224. https://doi.org/10.1016/j.chiabu.2009.12.003.

3   Schimel, J., Greenberg, J., Martens, A. (2003). Evidence That Projection of a Feared Trait Can Serve a Defensive Function. *Personality and Social Psychology Bulletin*. 29(8):969–979. doi: 10.1177/0146167203252969.

Playbook Move 24: Recognize When You Are the Weakest Link

1   Galford, R., Frisch, B., Greene, C. (2015). *Simple Sabotage: A Modern Field Manual for Detecting and Rooting Out Everyday Behaviors.* New York: HarperCollins Publishing.

Playbook Move 25: Consider the Risks of Acting Responsibly

1   Zucker, R. (April 17, 2019). Why Highly Efficient Leaders Fail. *Harvard Business Review.* https://hbr.org/2019/02/why-highly-efficient-leaders-fail.

Playbook Move 26: Link Their Success to Your Survival

1   Kim, E., Glomb, T. M. (2014). Victimization of High Performers: The Roles of Envy and Work Group Identification. *Journal of Applied Psychology*. 99(4):619. https://doi.org/10.1037/a0035789.

2   Reh, S., Tröster, C., Van Quaquebeke, N. (2018). Keeping (Future) Rivals Down: Temporal Social Comparison Predicts Coworker Social Undermining via Future Status Threat and Envy. *Journal of Applied Psychology*. 103(4):399. https://doi.org/10.1037/apl0000281.

3 Grant, A. M. (2013). *Give and Take: A Revolutionary Approach to Success*. New York: Penguin.

Playbook Move 27: Don't Be Captivated by Charisma

1 Brunell, A. B., Gentry, W. A., Campbel, W. K., Hoffman, B. J., Kuhnert, K. W., DeMarree, K. G. (2008). Leader Emergence: The Case of the Narcissistic Leader. *Personality and Social Psychology Bulletin*. 34(12):1663–1676. https://doi.org/10.1177/0146167208324101.

2 Woodman, T., Akehurst S., Hardy, L., Beattie, S. (2010). Self-Confidence and Performance: A Little Self-Doubt Helps. *Psychology of Sport and Exercise*. 11(6):467–470. https://doi.org/10.1016/j.psychsport.2010.05.009.

3 Chamorro-Premuzic, T. (2019). *Why Do So Many Incompetent Men Become Leaders? (And How to Fix It)* . Boston: Harvard Business Press.

4 Grabo, A., Spisak, B. R., van Vugt, M. (2017). Charisma as Signal: An Evolutionary Perspective on Charismatic Leadership. *The Leadership Quarterly*. 28(4):473–485. https://doi.org/10.1016/j.leaqua.2017.05.001.

5 Mayo, M. (2017). If Humble People Make the Best Leaders, Why Do We Fall For Charismatic Narcissists? *Harvard Business Review*. https://hbr.org/2017/04/if-humble-people-make-the-best-leaders-why-do-we-fall-for-charismatic-narcissists.

6 Owens, B. P., Hekman, D. R. (2016). How Does Leader Humility Influence Team Performance? Exploring the Mechanisms of Contagion and Collective Promotion Focus. *Academy of Management Journal*. 59(3):1088–1111. https://doi.org/10.5465/amj.2013.0660.

7 Hermalin, B. E. (October 2, 2014). At the Helm, Kirk or Spock? The Pros and Cons of Charismatic Leadership. *SSRN*. http://dx.doi.org/10.2139/ssrn.2419586.

Playbook Move 29: Be Better Than Your Backstabbers

1 Su, A. J. (November 22, 2016). How to Handle a Colleague Who's a Jerk When the Boss Isn't Around. *Harvard Business Review*. https://hbr.org/2016/11/how-to-handle-a-colleague-whos-a-jerk-when-the-boss-isnt-around.

1   Pojasek, R. B. (2000). Asking "Why?" Five Times. *Environmental Quality Management.* 10(1):79–84. https://doi.org/10.1002/1520-6483(200023)10:1<79::AID-TQEM10>3.0.CO;2-H.

2   Love, J. (September 7, 2016). Don't Wait to Be Asked: Lead. *Kellogg Insight.* https://insight.kellogg.northwestern.edu/article/dont-wait-to-be-asked-lead.

Playbook Move 31: Own the Language

1   Kurtz, J. (January 16, 2019). GOP Insiders Knock Their Depictions in New Dick Cheney Biopic "Vice." *The Hill.* https://thehill.com/blogs/in-the-know/in-the-know/425538-gop-insiders-knock-their-depictions-in-new-dick-cheney-biopic.

2   Press, T. A. (January 21, 2007). George A. Smathers, 93, Dies: Former Senator from Florida. https://www.nytimes.com/2007/01/21/us/21smathers.html.

Playbook Move 32: Mimic Their Moves

1   Iacoboni, M. (2008). *Mirroring People: The New Science of How We Connect with Others.* New York: Picador.

2   Pineda, J. (2007). *Mirror Neuron Systems: The Role of Mirroring Processes in Social Cognition.* Atlanta, GA: Emory University. 191–212.

3   Talley, L., Temple, S. (2015). How Leaders Influence Followers through the Use of Nonverbal Communication. *Leadership & Organization Development Journal.* 36(1):69–80. https://doi.org/10.1108/LODJ-07-2013-0107.

4   Vecchi, G. M., Van Hasselt, V. B., Romano, S. J. (2005). Crisis (Hostage) Negotiation: Current Strategies and Issues in High-Risk Conflict Resolution. *Aggression and Violent Behavior.* 10(5):533–551. https://doi.org/10.1016/j.avb.2004.10.001.

5   Keirsey, D., Bates M. M. (1984). *Please Understand Me.* Del Mar, CA: Prometheus Nemesis.

6   Keirsey, D. (1998). *Please Understand Me II.* Del Mar, CA: Prometheus Nemesis.

7   Markova, D., McArthur, A. (2015). *Collaborative Intelligence.* New York: Random House.

8 Keirsey, D. (1998).

9 Keirsey, D. (1998).

10 Keirsey, D. (1998).

11 Keirsey, D. (1998).

Playbook Move 33: How to Complain

1 Leetaru, K. (September 4, 2018). Customer Service in the Social Media Era: Complain Publicly or Get Nothing. *Forbes*. https://www. forbes.com/sites/kalevleetaru/2018/09/04/customer-service-in-the-social-media-era-complain-publicly-or-get-nothing/#5a06f4725b09.

Playbook Move 34: Manage Your Meetings

1 Nembhard, I. M., Edmondson, A. C. (2006). Making It Safe: The Effects of Leader Inclusiveness and Professional Status on Psychological Safety and Improvement Efforts in Health Care Teams. *Journal of Organizational Behavior: The International Journal of Industrial, Occupational and Organizational Psychology and Behavior*. 27(7):941–966. https://doi.org/10.1002/job.413.

2 Delizonna, L. (August 24, 2017). High-Performing Teams Need Psychological Safety. Here's How to Create It. *Harvard Business Review*. 24.

3 Deng, C. (August 11, 2017). Are Men Talking Too Much? #whotalks Will Show You. Gender Avenger. https://www.genderavenger.com/blog/are-men-talking-too-much.

4 Rueckert, V. (2019). *Outspoken: Why Women's Voices Get Silenced and How to Set Them Free*. New York: HarperBusiness.

Playbook Move 35: Determine Whether the Problem Comes from Slackers or Structure

1 Peter, L. J., Hull, R. (1969). *The Peter Principle*. New York: William Morrow.

2 Parkinson, C. N. (1957). *Parkinson's Law and Other Studies in Administration*. Boston, MA: Houghton Mifflin.

3 Dunning, D. (2011). The Dunning-Kruger Effect: On Being Ignorant of One's Own Ignorance. *Advances in Experimental Social*

Psychology. 44:247–296. https://doi.org/10.1016/B978-0-12-385522-0.00005-6.

4 Chamorro-Premuzic, T. (2019). *Why Do So Many Incompetent Men Become Leaders? (And How to Fix It)*. Boston: Harvard Business Press.

5 Belmi, P., Neale, M. A., Reiff, D., Ulfe, R. (2019). The Social Advantage of Miscalibrated Individuals: The Relationship between Social Class and Overconfidence and Its Implications for Class-Based Inequality. *Journal of Personality and Social Psychology*. http://dx.doi.org/10.1037/pspi0000207.

6 Goodhart, C. (2015). Goodhart's Law. *The Encyclopedia of Central Banking*. Cheltenham, UK: Edward Elgar Publishing. 227.

7 Latané, B., Williams, K., Harkins, S. (1979). Many Hands Make Light the Work: The Causes and Consequences of Social Loafing. *Journal of Personality and Social Psychology*. 37(6):822. https://doi.org/10.1037/0022-3514.37.6.822.

8 Grivas, C., Puccio, G. J. (2012). *The Innovative Team*. San Francisco, CA: Jossey-Bass Publishers.

9 Dommeyer, C. J. (2007). Using the Diary Method to Deal With Social Loafers on the Group Project: Its Effects on Peer Evaluations, Group Behavior, and Attitudes. *Journal of Marketing Education*. 29(2):175–188. https://doi.org/10.1177/0273475307302019.

Playbook Move 37: Watch Your Back When You're in Charge

1 Pink, D. H. (2011). *Drive: The Surprising Truth about What Motivates Us*. New York: Penguin.

2 Scott, K. (2019). *Radical Candor: How to Get What You Want by Saying What You Mean*. United Kingdom: Pan Macmillan.

3 Stone, D., Patton, B., Heen, S., Fisher, R. (2011). *Difficult Conversations: How to Discuss What Matters Most*. London: Portfolio Penguin.

4 Stone, D., Heen, S. (2015). *Thanks for the Feedback: The Science and Art of Receiving Feedback Well (Even When It Is Off Base, Unfair, Poorly Delivered, and, Frankly, You're Not in the Mood)*. London: Portfolio Penguin.

5 Henderson, E. (2018). Inspirational Leadership: Hitler And Gandhi—Avoiding the Corrosive Power of Corruption. In: *Psychoanalytic Essays on Power and Vulnerability*. New York: Routledge. 85–108.

Playbook Move 38: Own the Mess You've Inherited

1 Baker, P. (June 12, 2009). Blaming the Guy Who Came before Doesn't Work Long. *New York Times*. https://www.nytimes.com/2009/06/12/us/politics/12memo.html.

2 Carucci, R. (January 19, 2018). Leading Effectively When You Inherit a Mess. *Harvard Business Review*. https://hbr.org/2017/08/leading-effectively-when-you-inherit-a-mess.

3 Shoup, M. (March 30, 2015). How to Turn Around a Failing Organization. *Inc.* https://www.inc.com/how-to-turn-around-a-failing-organization.html.

4 Sommer, S. A., Howell, J. M., Hadley, C. N. (2016). Keeping Positive and Building Strength: The Role of Affect and Team Leadership in Developing Resilience during an Organizational Crisis. *Group & Organization Management*. 41(2):172–202. https://doi.org/10.1177/1059601115578027.

Playbook Move 39: Beware of the Bobbleheads

1 Sanaghan, P., Goldstein, L. (March 30, 2015). The Seduction of the Leader. *Inside Higher Ed*. https://www.insidehighered.com/advice/2011/05/27/essay_on_college_leaders_and_the_advice_they_receive.

2 Prendergast, C. (1993). A Theory of "Yes Men." *The American Economic Review*. 83(4):757–770. www.jstor.org/stable/2117577.

3 Sanaghan. (2011).

Playbook Move 40: Don't Confuse Yourself with a Messiah

1 Barczak, G., Lassk, F., Mulki, J. (2010). Antecedents of Team Creativity: An Examination of Team Emotional Intelligence, Team Trust and Collaborative Culture. *Creativity and Innovation Management*. 19(4):332–345. https://doi.org/10.1111/j.1467-8691.2010.00574.x.

2 Cooperrider, D. L., Srivastva, S. (1987). Appreciative Inquiry in Organizational Life. In: Pasmore W, Woodman R, eds. *Research in Organizational Change and Development*. Greenwich, CT: JAI Press. 129–169.

3 Watkins, M. D. (2016). Leading the Team You Inherit. *Harvard Business Review*. 94(6):60–67.

Playbook Move 41: Pause before Killing the Cubs

1 Packer, E., Pusey, A. (1984). Infanticide in Carnivores. In: Hausfater G, Hardy SB, eds. *Infanticide: Comparative and Evolutionary Perspectives*. New York: Aldine. 31–42.

Playbook Move 42: Recognize the Difference between Aversion to Loss and Resistance to Change

1 Jansen, K. J. (2000). The Emerging Dynamics of Change: Resistance, Readiness, and Momentum. *People and Strategy*. 23(2):53.

2 Dent, E. B., Goldberg, S. G. (1999). Challenging "Resistance to Change." *The Journal of Applied Behavioral Science*. 35(1):25–41. https://doi.org/10.1177/0021886399351003.

Playbook Move 43: Create the Right Coalition

1 Pach, C. J. (July 26, 2017). Dwight D. Eisenhower: Impact and Legacy. https://millercenter.org/president/eisenhower/impact-and-legacy.

2 Bacharach, S. B. (2018). *Agenda Mover: When Your Good Idea Is Not Enough*. Ithaca: Cornell University Press.

3 Robinson, S. (April 12, 2012). 6 People You Need to Start a Revolution. *AlterNet*. https://www.alternet.org/2012/04/6_people_you_need_to_start_a_revolution.

4 Hindman, H. D. (2016). *Child Labor: An American History*. New York: Routledge.

5 Kreps, D. (July 8, 2016). Hear Jay Z Tackle Police Brutality on Raw New Song "Spiritual." *Rolling Stone*. https://www.rollingstone.com/music/music-news/hear-jay-z-tackle-police-brutality-on-raw-new-song-spiritual-165528/.

6 Cobb, J. (November 27, 2019). The Powerful Perspective of "Queen & Slim." *The New Yorker*. https://www.newyorker.com/culture/cultural-comment/the-powerful-perspective-of-queen-and-slim.

7   Vischer, M. (July 3, 2020). How Long Is 8:46 In Classical Music? Musicians Honor George Floyd with Moving 'Albinoni Adagio.' CPR Classical. https://www.cpr.org/2020/07/03/how-long-is-846-in-classical-music-musicians-honor-george-floyd-with-moving-albinoni-adagio/.

8   Lasher, M. (June 27, 2019). Read the Full Transcript of Jesse Williams' Powerful Speech on Race at the BET Awards. *TIME*. https://time.com/4383516/jesse-williams-bet-speech-transcript/.

Playbook Move 44: Replace Your Answers with Questions

1   Garvin, D. A., Roberto, M. A. (2001). What You Don't Know about Making Decisions. *Harvard Business Review.* 79(8):108–119.

2   Ross, R., Roberts, C. (1994). Balancing Advocacy and Inquiry. In: Senge, P., Kleiner, A., Roberts, C., Ross, R., Smith, B., eds. *The Fifth Discipline Fieldbook.* New York: Doubleday. 253–259.

3   Schein, E. H. (2014). *Humble Inquiry: The Gentle Art of Asking Instead of Telling.* San Francisco: Berrett-Koehler Publishers, Inc.

4   Schein. (2014).

5   Productive Conversations: Using Advocacy and Inquiry Effectively. (December 31, 2015) https://thesystemsthinker.com/productive-conversations-using-advocacy-and-inquiry-effectively/.

6   McArthur, P. W. (2014). Advocacy and Inquiry. In: Coughlin D, Brydon-Miller, eds. *The Sage Encyclopedia of Action Research.* Los Angeles: Sage Publishing. 26–29.

Playbook Move 45: Stop Silencing the Skeptics

1   Mariana, P., Violeta, S. (2011). Opportunity to Reduce Resistance to Change in a Process of Organizational Change. *Annals of the University of Oradea, Economic Science Series.* 20(2):698–702. http://anale.steconomiceuoradea.ro/volume/2011/n2/099.pdf.

2   Heifetz, R., Linsky, M. (2017). *Leadership on the Line: Staying Alive through the Dangers of Change.* Boston: Harvard Business Press.

3   Kanter, R. M. (September 25, 2012). Ten Reasons People Resist Change. *Harvard Business Review.* https://hbr.org/2012/09/ten-reasons-people-resist-change.

4 Dent, E. B., Goldberg, S. G. (1999). Challenging "Resistance to Change." *The Journal of Applied Behavioral Science*. 35(1):25–41. https://doi.org/10.1177/0021886399351003.

5 Porter, J., Gallo, A. (May 18, 2016). How to Handle the Naysayer on Your Team. *Harvard Business Review*. https://hbr.org/2016/03/how-to-handle-the-naysayer-on-your-team.

6 Grant, A. (March 8, 2019). Frustrated at Work? That Might Just Lead to Your Next Breakthrough. *New York Times*. https://www.nytimes.com/2019/03/08/smarter-living/frustrated-at-work-that-might-just-lead-to-your-next-breakthrough.html.

7 Bodell, L. (2012). *Kill the Company: End the Status Quo, Start an Innovation Revolution*. Brookline, MA: Bibliomotion.

Playbook Move 46: Exit before They Can Fire You

1 Stybel, L. J., Peabody, M. (2001). The Right Way to Be Fired. *Harvard Business Review*. 79(7):86–99.

2 Cain, Á. (January 8, 2019). 19 Signs You're about to Lose Your Job. *Business Insider*. https://www.businessinsider.com/subtle-signs-you-are-about-to-be-fired-2018-1.

Playbook Move 47: Be Prepared to Walk Away

1 Chen, J., White, B. (January 8, 2019). What Are Best Practices Relating to Counter-Offers? Cornell University, ILR School. https://digitalcommons.ilr.cornell.edu/student/194.

Playbook Move 50: Do Your Part to Reduce Organizational Politics

1 Chang, C. H., Rosen, C. C., Levy, P. E. (2009). The Relationship between Perceptions of Organizational Politics and Employee Attitudes, Strain, and Behavior: A Meta-Analytic Examination. *Academy of Management Journal*. 52(4):779–801. www.jstor.org/stable/40390316.

2 Rosen, C. C., Levy, P. E., Hall, R. J. (2006). Placing Perceptions of Politics in the Context of the Feedback Environment, Employee Attitudes, and Job Performance. *Journal of Applied Psychology*. 91(1):211. https://doi.org/10.1037/0021-9010.91.1.211.

3 Scott, K. (2019). *Radical Candor: How to Get What You Want by Saying What You Mean.* United Kingdom: Pan Macmillan.

4 Wilkinson, A., Fay, C. (2011). New Times for Employee Voice? *Human Resource Management.* 50(1):65–74. https://doi.org/10.1002/hrm.20411.

5 Vogelgesang, G. R., Leroy, H., Avolio, B. J. (2013). The Mediating Effects of Leader Integrity with Transparency in Communication and Work Engagement/Performance. *The Leadership Quarterly.* 24(3):405–413. https://doi.org/10.1016/j.leaqua.2013.01.004.

6 Kark, R., Carmeli, A. (2009). Alive and Creating: The Mediating Role of Vitality and Aliveness in the Relationship between Psychological Safety and Creative Work Involvement. *Journal of Organizational Behavior: The International Journal of Industrial, Occupational and Organizational Psychology and Behavior.* 30(6):785–804. https://doi.org/10.1002/job.571.

Printed in Great Britain
by Amazon

45311920R00158